Living The Abundant Life

Adjusting Your Mindset and Finances to Live the Life You've Always Desired

Scott Ferguson JD, MBA, CFP®, ChFC®, CKA®–Founder/Wealth Advisor of Abundant Life Financial

D1519463

STREAMLINE
BOOKS

LIVING THE ABUNDANT LIFE

Adjusting Your Mindset and Finances to Live the Life You've Always Desired

Copyright © 2023 by Scott Ferguson

All rights reserved.

Cover Design by Will Severns

Streamline Books

www.WriteMyBooks.com

Paperback ISBN: 9-798-3700-2527-3

Hardcover ISBN:

February 1st, 2023

Contents

To my wonderful wife, Angela, along with my amazing children, Elle Louise and Otto. You bring abundant joy and adventure into my life —I love you all dearly.

To my parents, Steve & Jan. Thank you for always encouraging me in life and in my faith. You've always been an amazing example of what the Abundant Life looks like.

"I came that they may have life and have it abundantly."

John 10:10b (ESV)

Chapter 1

Setting the Stage

Growing up in rural Minnesota, I thought I had it all: a loving family, a quality education, and a basketball highlight reel that would rival Michael Jordan (alright, so that last one is a bit of a stretch). But we did win some basketball games in high school, and I also found joy and success in activities such as track, football, and band. My hometown was surrounded by lakes and, in the summer, nothing was better than spending time on the water and around a campfire. In the winter, our downtown looked like it belonged in a Hallmark movie—decorated beautifully for Christmas.

I had amazing coaches and friends. Even

the parents of my friends were like extensions of my family. Like many kids growing up in the American midwest, I didn't have many worries because life seemed well and good. Whether you call it, "privileged," or, "blessed," I look back now and recognize it was a bit of both.

When it came time for college, I chose the University of Minnesota. I went there on a track scholarship and for the great academics. They had just won the Big Ten Conference Championship for track and field, so I was excited to join a great team and compete at the highest level. I was enthusiastic about my future and ready to give it my all athletically and academically.

During my first week on campus, all athletes were required to take a physical/medical assessment. No big deal—I had taken plenty of them throughout my time in athletics. They scheduled the track team at the same time, but I couldn't go then because it was in the middle of one of my classes. I ended up having my physical at the same time as the entire softball team. Since I was a last-minute add-in, I had to wait three hours until the softball team was finished. It's worth noting my dad was a family physician in a small town. I'd never really sat in a waiting room that long before. After sitting for three hours with little to do, I was tired and about ready to go back to the dorm.

"Scott Ferguson, you're up next," said the nurse.

When I finally saw the doctor, he was distracted and finishing his notes from the previous patient. While writing at the desk in his exam room, we made small talk. He was not very intent on my exam.

What event do you run in track? What does your mom do? How about your dad?

He asked me these questions about life and the small talk continued, but I was just tired and wanted to get the assessment over with. When I told him my dad was a family practice physician, the whole tone of the exam immediately changed.

He put his pen down and turned around to face me.

"What was that? Your dad's a doctor?"

When I said he was, he immediately started the exam.

I was in the office for over an hour for a sports physical. Every little thing he found, he'd say, "I bet your dad didn't know that." I reminded him my dad wasn't MY doctor. It didn't seem to matter. "Your feet pronate. I bet your dad didn't know that."

It went on and on. More than 20 years later, I still believe he was the most arrogant person I've ever met. Eventually, he found a tiny bump on my neck. "You've got a small lump on your neck. It could be cancerous. I bet your dad didn't know that."

By the time he said those words, my tired freshman self was fed up. I had already been there for four hours and had enough of his poor bedside manner. I told him, "You win. My dad doesn't know that, and I've already put in an order for your trophy. It should show up next week. I think we're done here."

But he wouldn't let up. "Nope, it really could be cancerous, Scott," he said, "You're going to have to stay and do some blood work."

If I thought waiting for the softball team took a long time, the blood work felt just as long (keep in mind, this is before cell phones).

After five hours in total, a bizarre interaction with the doctor, and a newfound health scare that was totally news to me . . . I was finally allowed to leave.

For the next two or three weeks, I had to submit to a variety of tests. I told my coach they were just standard from my physical assessment a few weeks prior. Sure, maybe cancer *was* a possibility, but nothing in my life had really gone wrong before . . . So why should I be worried? I ended up seeing an Ear, Nose, and Throat specialist. At first, he couldn't find the lump. When he *did find it*, he said, "I can barely feel that. I'm not even sure I'd call it a lump, but I guess we can check it out."

He did a needle biopsy in my neck to pull cells that would be tested for cancer. He then asked if his medical student could take a sample as well. Since I'm a lover of science, I gave him a thumbs up—even found the process until that point pretty fascinating. But when his student placed the long needle in my neck, the pain was *excruciating*. The needle felt more like a steak knife, and it was the moment in my life I remember liking science a little less.

A few days later, I got a phone call from my parents. My mom began with a very somber tone. "Scott, I have to tell you something. We got a call from the doctor today . . . You do indeed have cancer."

I laughed—it was a defense mechanism. And my mom, who is the most positive, upbeat, and supportive person I've ever met said, "Scott, this is no time to laugh. This is serious."

"Well crying and moping won't make it go away," I said.

We both sat in silence for a moment over the phone. Laughter gave way to confusion, which gave way to a moment for me to think about my whole life—as a freshman, as an athlete, and as a student with my whole life ahead.

"I'm going to approach this with a positive attitude, Mom," I responded, "And whatever God has in store for me, I'm at peace with. Whatever happens will happen."

There was a part of me that laughed inside because, of course, that jerk of a doctor was right (and, in hindsight, I'm amazed how God used his arrogance to help me!). But the main reason I laughed was the overwhelming calm I experienced. I was so struck by the abundant love I felt from God that I couldn't explain it. I could only laugh.

The formal diagnosis was thyroid cancer, and the tumor ended up being less than a centimeter in diameter. The cool thing about the thyroid is it absorbs all the iodine in your body (okay, so I still geek out over science from time to time). The absorption allows doctors to give patients radioactive iodine to kill the cancer cells. The iodine even works to hunt and kill other thyroid cancer cells throughout the body and helps the scan light up to see if the radioactive particles went where they were supposed to go. When they gave me the radioactive iodine, there were no less than three doctors and five medical students in the room. Thinking it a bit overkill, I put on my most serious face and asked, "How long will I be glowing?" I only managed to get one med student to crack a smile. The other doctors weren't having it, and I was reminded again, like my mother before, that some things *weren't* a laughing matter.

Luckily, the cancer had not spread—allowing the doctors to perform surgery and remove it. Before surgery, the surgeon told me mine was his final surgery after a long career. As I shook his hand, it was trembling. I looked at him with a little fear in my eyes. He smiled, gripped my hand tightly, and assured me he would take good care of me. He did just that —his final surgery was a success and the scar left behind was minimal. After the surgery, I had another dose of radioactive iodine to kill the cells the doctors weren't able to remove. Ultimately, it was caught so early that the years that followed, thankfully, left me with little cause to worry.

My cancer story and experience left me with a different kind of education I never expected as a freshman at the University of Minnesota. To put it mildly, the months of September to October 2000 changed my whole outlook on life. I realized Christianity wasn't just something I believed in—it was my whole hope and identity. In that dark moment of my life, there was a light that went so much deeper than my feeble attempts at laughter. Cancer was the darkest news I could have received in that first year, yet in it I found peace. I began to understand my life was aimed toward eternity–not death. And you know what else? I began to understand eternity was infinitely better than a "good" midwestern life and upbringing.

All the worldly stress I felt in college just didn't matter anymore. My moments in this life were part of a bigger story–not THE story. I had to make the most of each opportunity as I received it. The words of Philippians 4:7 became a reality in my life: "And the peace of God, which surpasses all understanding, will guard your hearts and your minds in Christ Jesus" (ESV). Once I shook that doctor's trembling hand, and he performed a successful surgery, I committed the remainder of my life to the impact I could have on people.

In the years that followed, I had a wonderful college experience. Our track team won the Big Ten Championship, and I got a nice, big championship ring. To go from high school state hurdle champion, to doctors saying I wouldn't have the energy to compete, to finishing in the top 10 of the Big Ten and being part of a championship team was quite the journey. But the best part of college was the friends and memories I made along the way. After graduation, I went to law school, then eventually set off on a career path as a wealth advisor. One of the best parts of my career has been the inspiration I've found from clients. I've had thousands of meetings with people–many who are multimillionaires and others who have very little. Each of them has taught me so much about how to live life and approach finances. They have shown me that living an abundant life is not determined by the amount of money you make. Although some are solely focused on earning the almighty dollar, they don't realize more money won't bring them true joy. My experience is that your mindset is what ultimately drives joy.

In the book of Ecclesiastes, King Solomon details how he had it all–money, women, possessions, and I'm sure plenty of savings in his 401(k)! Ultimately, he concluded none of these things made him happy. Instead, he found true joy and abundance were rooted in God. Spiritual, financial, and psychological abundance comes from knowing you are part of God's family and that He is *for* you. The antithesis of worry is joy; the abundant life is more joy and less worry.

Have you ever been in two houses with the same square footage but one seems bigger than the other? Oftentimes, it is because the house that seems smaller has space allocated to unimportant areas. These space grabbers make the whole house seem cramped. This same principle can be applied to our lives. Two people may have similar jobs, homes, and families. Yet one seems joyful, fun, adventurous, and full while the other seems stressful, worried, and empty. While they both have the same square footage, one may just need some rearranging.

It can be difficult to challenge your core belief that money and possessions bring happiness and to realize it is *God* who must fill those voids in your life. However, it is only by doing so you can become the person who is filled with joy, fun, and adventure. I'm not saying you don't need money or that the actions you take don't matter. Those things are important. But before focusing on them, you need to take a moment and ask, why? Why do these things seem to matter to me? Why do I feel I need this to be happy?

Society needs good people to make money and do good things with it. I'm a big believer that the harder you work, the luckier you get and there are many verses in Proverbs that discuss the importance of hard work. But don't do it for the sake of chasing a mirage. If you put "making money" over everything else and miss out on family and friends, then what good is it? Even if you win the rat race, you're still a rat. Stop and think about your life plan as we each are given only *one* life to live (that's the REAL number to focus on). Money is a tool we use to reach an end. Don't get your self-worth from your net worth. Remember God, in his infinite wisdom, leaves room to have fun along the way as well.

I hope this book serves as a similar wake-up call to the one I had as a college freshman. I hope it will cause you to take a moment and say, "Hold on. Is this the life that I have always wanted?" There are so many decisions people make, consciously or unconsciously, to "keep up with the Joneses." They make decisions because that's "just what people do." I hope you will stop and consider what is truly important—a life of intention and impact. The power of patience can make all the difference, and you might even find (like I did) that there *is* immense joy even in the waiting.

While this may all seem rather simplified, I have found it to be true. If you find more joy, you have less worry. I love Kay Warren's definition of joy from her book *Choose Joy*, which states, "Joy is a settled assurance that God is in control of all the details of my life, the quiet confidence that ultimately everything is going to be all right, and a determined choice to praise God in all things." If you want to have a truly abundant life, you have to change how you think about life and money. My cancer experience has shaped my belief about life and living it to its fullest. That's not to say dark moments and sorrow don't come–because I certainly have my share. But with a change in mindset, you can live the life you've always wanted to live.

When you see someone living an Abundant Life in real life, it's truly a special thing. From the wonderful people in my life, I've learned a bit more about what it takes to change my mindset and strategy about money. Their example has helped me make a list of common themes to share about getting on the path toward a fuller life.

Changing your mindset isn't necessarily easy. After each chapter, ask yourself, "What did I take away from that chapter? What changes do I need to explore? Who should I partner with to ensure I get on the right path?" As you read through these pages, I hope you find your way to a life filled with more abundance and joy than you ever thought possible.

Journey Towards An Abundant Life

1. **A**ppreciate What You Have
2. **B**elieve Everything Is God's
3. **U**nderstand Where You're Headed
4. **N**avigate Your Short and Long-Term Plans
5. **D**evelop a Strategy for Risk
6. **A**cknowledge the Past. Find Joy in the Present. Prepare for the Future.
7. **N**urture Others
8. **T**ake Time for the People in Your Life
9. **LIFE**–Live Your LIFE with Joy

For Reflection

1. Has there been a time when your whole outlook on life changed? What caused the change and how did you see God working through it?
2. Thinking back on your life, what has brought you the most joy?
3. Are you living the life you have always wanted? If not, what could you change to make that happen?

"For I have learned to be content whatever the circumstances."

Philippians 4:11b

Chapter 2

Appreciate What You Have

*S o many people focus on what they don't
have.* Take Adam and Eve, for example.
They lived in a wonderful garden. It wasn't
exactly Minnesota, but they had everything.
No worries. No pain. All the food they could
eat. An intimate relationship with God. Who
could ask for more? And yet, they *did* want
more. They wanted the one thing they
couldn't have. They began to focus on that
and then could see nothing else. They
stopped appreciating what they DID have
and began longing for what they DIDN'T
have. Having the wrong focus led to worry,
jealousy and fear.

When I was a child, I remember thinking,

"Why did Adam and Eve screw everything up?" It seemed so obvious. All they had to do was to cherish the abundance they already had in their lives instead of the one little thing they didn't possess—the "knowledge of good and evil." But the devil is sneaky. He is the master of lies and promoting fear and worry. He knew by taking their eyes off of God it would cause their downfall. And that is exactly what happened.

It is easy for the same thing to happen to us. We put together a 1,000-piece puzzle, but when we get to the end, there is one piece missing. We tend to focus on the missing piece instead of the 999 pieces that were there. We say to ourselves, "What a waste of time!" because we couldn't finish it all— instead of seeing the joy we found from putting the pieces together. With everyone sharing their new home, their amazing vacation, and their other material possessions on social media, it's easy to feel like we're missing quite a few puzzle pieces.

How can we keep our eyes on God *in addition* to the abundance in our lives without letting worry and fear overtake us? I had a mentor once tell me, "If things aren't right in your business, you've got to go upstream. If you're not right with God, you're not right with yourself. If you're not right with yourself, you're not right with your family. If you're not right with your family, you're not right with your clients." I've often gone back to his advice. When I start to worry, I start looking "upstream."

In the lead-up to writing this book, I had to make an important decision that would change the course of my business. Initially, I was excited about the change and sure it was the right direction. Then it hit me. What if this change does not go well? Am I taking too much risk? Is this the right decision? I was worried and it was easy to focus on the worst-case scenario. Then I thought back to my friend's advice. I centered my thoughts on God instead of my situation. I focused on familiar song lyrics, "Lord, I need you. Oh, I need you. Every hour I need you."

That song must have played 30 times through my speakers one night. It helped me focus on God. It made me realize I can't do this on my own; I don't have to do it myself.

God is there with me *every hour* despite life's risks and uncertainties. What a relief!

After finding peace with God, I prioritized routines and rhythms to take care of myself and relieve stress. I spent more time exercising and eating better. I prioritized time with my wife and played with my kids. By focusing on God, good habits, and family, I was able to find peace again. I've found that when I focus too much on the negative, I must replace those thoughts with positive, meaningful ones.

How can you make sure you are right with God, with yourself, your family, and others? It is only when we draw close to God that we realize how big HE is and how small EVERYTHING else is!

I am fortunate to have seen examples of the abundant life in my own family. My father's parents were incredible people that were active in their church and community; they lived on a farm and had a great life surrounded by close family and friends. My mom's parents were married for 78 years and were 104 and 99 years old respectively when they passed. I used to joke that Grandpa

Hank single-handedly killed the pension system because he received a check longer than his working years.

With only a modest income, they taught me you don't have to be rich to live rich lives. Grandpa Hank started as a blue-collar worker and worked his way up the corporate ladder at Northwestern Bell. By setting priorities and not spending money on unimportant things, he was able to build a small lake cabin where our family could go to relax and make memories. Grandma loved tennis. By focusing on her passion, she was able to remain active and win a tennis tournament at age 83. She even took her bucket list trip to Wimbledon. Grandpa was still playing golf on his 100th birthday. One time, when he was 98, I called him randomly. He answered saying, "I'm at the gym, I'll call you back." Then, he proceeded to hang up on me! Later, he did call back and said that he was doing leg presses and wasn't happy with his performance. He vowed to get his strength back by the end of the year and was coming up with a plan to do so when I called. Without prioritizing the important things in their lives, none of this would have been possible.

My grandparents didn't live fancy lives but instead allocated money that aligned with what they cared about. They came to all my sporting events and were always my biggest cheerleaders. My friends always enjoyed Grandpa Hank's next-level dad jokes that came from the wisdom of being a dad for a long time. I once asked Grandpa the secret to such longevity. He smiled and said, "I live in Fargo, North Dakota. So, for about 3-6 months of the year, I'm cryogenically frozen. In Fargo years, I'm really only 70!" It was the perfect Grandpa Hank response. My Grandma's answer was a little more straightforward and respected all the same.

When I saw Grandma the last time before she passed, I asked her if she had any advice for me–anything she had learned from life and would be willing to share. She said, "Always strive for balance. Work hard, but not so hard that you don't see your family. Eat well, but always eat cake on your birthday." Their example of an abundant life has reverberated throughout each component of our family.

My grandparents focused on what was important and understood that happiness doesn't come from having more possessions. Have you come to that realization in your life? Maybe you don't need as much stuff as you think you do! Are you aligning your assets with your priorities? Have you considered the joy and freedom you might have by letting go of unnecessary things to make room for what is truly important?

Jesus helped his disciples understand he was God incarnate by telling them parables– simple stories with deep meaning. Because most of his followers were hard-working people, many of his stories were about jobs and life experiences to which his audience could relate. One example is recorded in the gospel of John about the life and characteristics of a good shepherd.

Shepherds talked to the sheep and called them by name so much that the sheep recognized their voices and were willing to follow them almost anywhere. When wolves or other predators were trying to attack the flock, the shepherds fought for them and were willing to lay down their lives to protect them. They also defended the sheep from thieves and robbers who climbed over the fence to grab them. The shepherds were the gatekeepers for the sheep, standing at the entrance of the pen to oversee their coming and going. They often led them to pastures filled with green grass that would nourish them and help them grow stronger. Just like the good shepherd helped the sheep live a full life, Jesus said he also came so his followers could not only have life but an ABUN-DANT life.

We are the sheep, protected and cared for by Jesus. We do not need to focus on the worries of the world but rather focus on all that Jesus has provided already.

Consider what is truly important. What brings you joy? What are the things that fill you up? If you value your family and the way your family grows closer together is through travel, you might need a smaller home so you have more funds to explore the world. Instead of starting with possessions; start with lifestyle. Align your finances with what you value.

As a wealth advisor, I am always surprised at how much work it is to clean out a house after a loved one has passed. Most clients who have gone through the experience comment about how challenging it was to clean out mom and dad's home. Most homes are filled to the point of overflowing. Many people keep stuff they should have eliminated years ago. Why do we hang on to things we no longer need or use? It is often because we tend to value what we already have and find it wasteful to get rid of it.

Consider that everything you have belongs to God; it is only loaned to you for a little while. The things you may no longer need may be someone else's treasure. While you hate to get rid of it, having a cluttered home could add to the multitude of stress you already feel. Most folks end up leaving their children in the exact same place they were in when their parents passed. Except now they have a bigger home and more stuff!

As you consider your priorities, don't spend your time comparing yourself to others.

Comparison steals your joy. God understood the power of envy and it was so important that it was included in the Ten Commandments: "You shall not covet your neighbor's house; you shall not covet your neighbor's wife, ...or anything that is your neighbor's" (Exodus 20:17 ESV).

Growing up, one of my friends had a trampoline. I was so jealous of that trampoline. When his family was out of town, all of us neighborhood kids would sneak over to his house and jump on it. It was so much fun! Why did my friend get to have all the fun? Why couldn't I have a trampoline too? I spent so much time longing for what he had that I forgot to appreciate that I had an awesome yard that everyone used when we played football games. I also didn't realize there was a downside to the trampoline. My friend broke his arm at least twice while jumping on it. I was so consumed with jealousy of what I didn't have that I couldn't appreciate what I already had in my life.

Joy and abundance can be found in almost every situation. I recently returned to the

University of Minnesota dorm where I lived during college. I always loved the dorm life. Yet looking back, the conditions were pretty dreary. We had four sweaty guys all over 6' tall crammed in one room with a lot of furniture. We had four beds lofted, desks underneath, a TV, and an uncomfortable futon. Even though it was probably the most cramped living conditions I ever experienced, those are some of the happiest memories I have to date. I didn't need a designer dorm to be happy.

Gratitude is a muscle that needs to be exercised daily!

In an age riddled with social media and get-rich-quick schemes, it is easy to compare yourself to others. Sometimes it seems like everyone DOES have the perfect life. Yet, realistically, that is not the case. While the grass may look greener on the other side, you aren't seeing the hours spent sweating, watering, and mowing to keep it that way. Our family says prayers every night before we go to bed and intentionally go around and say what we are thankful for. Gratitude is a muscle that needs to be exercised daily!

Redefine what it means to have an abundant life and remind yourself happiness is not found in having more things. Recall God has a purpose and a plan for your life. It is when you begin to appreciate what you already have that you will have the freedom to live a life of abundance.

For Reflection

1. Part of appreciating what you have is about focusing on what you have vs what you do not. List 5 items in your life that you appreciate.
2. Daily gratitude leads to appreciating what you have more —what routines would you like to start around gratitude?
3. What ways have you found to draw close to God and realize how big HE is and how small EVERYTHING else is?

"But who am I, and who are my people, that we should be able to give as generously as this? Everything comes from you, and we have given you only what comes from your hand."

1 Chronicles 29:14

Chapter 3

Believe Everything Is God's

I f everything is God's, then *everything* you have, including your life, is a gift. Being alive is something to be appreciated because it isn't guaranteed. If you're alive, God has a purpose and a plan for your life!

Believing everything belongs to God is a concept rooted deeply in scripture. The book of Genesis tells of how God made everything, including a garden where he let the first people, Adam and Eve, live for a time. King David wrote of it in the Psalms when he said, "The earth is the Lord's and the fullness thereof, the world and those who dwell therein" (Psalm 24:1 ESV). God spoke through the prophets using a man named

Haggai, and said, "The silver is mine, and the gold is mine, declares the Lord of hosts" (Haggai 2:8 ESV).

The New Testament is also full of reminders that everything belongs to God and possessions are just on loan to us for a short time. The apostle John begins his gospel by stating, "Through him all things were made; without him nothing was made that has been made" (John 1:3). The apostle Paul also reminds readers, "What do you have that God hasn't given you? And if everything you have is from God, why boast as though it were not a gift" (1 Corinthians 4:7b NLT)?

God talks a lot about money. Depending on how you define it, the Bible mentions money over 2,300 times. God understood the desire to have more possessions could distract you from drawing closer to Him. Therefore, he gave the ultimate guidebook about dealing with our wealth. In the New Testament, the apostle Paul encouraged his friend Timothy to lead a godly life by being happy and content with what he had. He warned Timothy not to fall into the trap of putting the desire to have more over the desire to have a relationship with God. Paul told Timothy, "For the LOVE of money is a root of all kinds of evil" (1 Timothy 6:10a). Many like to change his words and say, "Money is the root of all evil." The Bible doesn't say that. Instead, the verse says loving money and putting the desire to have more above God can lead to downfall. Money is not bad or good – it is simply a tool. Evangelist Joseph Prince once said, "Use money and love people. Don't love money and use people."

Indiana Jones and the Last Crusade is one of my favorite action movies. Throughout the movie, Elsa is searching for the Holy Grail. In one of the movie's final scenes, Indiana Jones grabs Elsa's hand as she is dangling from a ledge. However, rather than giving Indiana both hands and letting him pull her to safety, Elsa uses one hand to reach for the Grail and ultimately falls to her death. She loved Indy, but she loved the Grail more.

Every time I watch the scene, I'm amazed at her decision. I tell myself I would never do the same. Yet, doesn't Elsa's story seem a bit like our relationship with God? He is reaching out His hand for us, but we allow ourselves to slip from His loving grasp because we value other things more. Are we really that much different from Elsa?

Believing everything belongs to God can revolutionize your life by making you focus on the *impact* of your money. Knowing that all things belong to Him makes it easier to give and to appreciate. The concept is the precursor to stewardship. Let's think for a minute . . .

If everything I earn is *mine,* then my tendency is to want to keep it for myself. However, if I know the money belongs to someone else, I tend to use it for the purpose as the other planned. If I focus on the fact that everything I own and earn comes from God, then I have a totally different mindset: what is God's plan and purpose for it?

I remember attending a Kingdom Advisors conference breakout session led by author, speaker, and pastor, John Maxwell. He retold Jesus' parable of the Good Samaritan–linking each character in the story to a money mindset. He used the robber to explain "what's yours is mine and I'm going to take it," the priest to exemplify "what's mine is mine and I'm going to keep it," and the Samaritan to show "what's mine is yours and I'm going to give it." He rounded out the talk by reminding the audience "what's mine is not mine and I'm going to steward it."

I was fascinated by Maxwell's interpretation of this well-known story but was even more intrigued by what he did at the end. He asked someone in the audience to give him $100. One guy raised his hand, went onstage, and gave him a hundred-dollar bill. Everyone was pretty amazed at the man's generosity until Maxwell told us that he had given the man the money before the session and told him when it was time to give it back. You see, it was much easier for that man to give generously because it was not his money to begin with.

Giving generously is easy to talk about but much harder to put into practice. When money is only passing through your hands and was never yours in the first place, it is easy to hold it with an open hand. However, when the money comes out of your paycheck, then our tendency is to start rationalizing. I can't give it now because I have to pay off some debt or save for a new home. I want to buy a larger television or a new cell phone. The list goes on and on.

Growing up in a small town, one of the highlights of my summer weekend was going to the car races. I didn't love the races, but I enjoyed the crashes. It was always fun to watch the cars careen recklessly around the well-worn dirt racetrack and then bang into each other. It was even more fun because I got to spend time with one of my best friends, Jeremy, and his amazing family.

I remember once when my dad reached into his pocket and pulled out a crisp $20 bill. He told me to go and have fun. It was awesome! Freedom and fun were mine for the taking. Dad expected me to spend a couple dollars for admission, buy a snack, and then bring the rest home as change. However, being the sweet tooth that I am, I couldn't resist the candy stand. When I passed by, I saw gum, chocolate, Sweet Tarts, and more. In that instant, my money seemed to burn a hole in my pocket. Without thinking, I spent the entire $20 on candy. When Dad came to pick me up, I had a stomach ache and a baseball cap full of candy.

As we get older, we often find ourselves in the same position. However, our candy gets more complicated. Our spending is dictated by how much money we have and our yearnings continue to keep up with our earnings. As we make more money, we find ourselves spending more on worldly possessions. We buy it all without considering the consequences. We spend first and save and give what's left over. What we find is there's little left to save or give because we spent first–like I did with the candy.

Believing all your possessions belong to God changes everything. It changes your obsessions and your need to have more. It makes you more appreciative. You have been entrusted with a gift from God, so how will you use it wisely?

God asks us to give first before using the rest as a reminder that it is not ours to begin with. How would it change your life if you were applying for a job and the hiring manager said, "This number will be your salary and this number is money we're paying you that we wish for you to give away to a worthy cause." It's a difference of mindset. It is not that I have to give away some of my money, but I have been given extra to give to others. Trust God has positive plans for you.

He knows the more you honor His plans for your life, the closer you draw to Him. The more you act on His plans the more you realize He loves you and wants what is best for you.

I've seen so many clients with the mindset of the apostle Paul. They have learned to be content whatever their circumstances. Unlike those constantly chasing after happiness from things, they find peace with where they are in life. It is such a beautiful thing when you see someone who has found true contentment; there is a peace about them as if a weight has been lifted. They look for joy in the journey rather than hoping to find it at the end of the road.

It is my relationships with clients that have inspired me to change my thinking about what God has given me. I hope you will let the understanding that everything belongs to God permeate your life.

By realizing God's role in your existence, you will begin to find peace and truly understand the blessing written about in Hebrews 13:5-6, which says, "Keep your lives free from the LOVE of money and be content with what you have, BECAUSE God has said, 'Never will I leave you; never will I forsake you.' So we say with CONFIDENCE, 'The Lord is my helper; I will not be afraid. What can mere mortals do to me?'"

For Reflection

1. How might believing *everything* you have, including your life, is a gift from God change the way you approach life?
2. Imagine you are applying for a job and the hiring manager says, "This number will be your salary and this number is money we're paying you that we wish for you to give away to a worthy cause." What cause would you choose to be your beneficiary? Why?

"'For I know the plans I have for you,' declares the Lord, 'plans to prosper you and not to harm you, plans to give you hope and a future.'"

Jeremiah 29:11

Chapter 4

Understand Where You're Headed

Where do you want to be in 10, 20, or 30 years? More importantly, what kind of person do you want to be in the future? What is the life you want to live? Do you want to be the person who gives freely and doesn't sweat the small stuff? Do you want your children to love you and WANT to spend time with you? Do you want to be in alignment with the path God has set for you?

Picture what your future self looks like and take steps *now* to become *that* kind of person. American author Zig Ziglar said, "If you aim for nothing, you'll hit it every time." Take the time to think about where you want your life to go. Don't wait till the end of life to become the best you. Life is a joyous journey that begins with one step forward.

Sometimes, when I lose sight of what the future version of myself looks like, I think of Jesus. How can I become a person who loves and thinks about others first? How can I be humble and willing to serve those around me? How can I have a life full of prayer and rejoicing while not being anxious about anything? How can I make these things a priority in my life?

These changes don't happen overnight. Change can be an entire process–a journey. It is not as if you suddenly become the person God made you to be, but you are navigating toward it. It is like a ship with a compass set on a course before the trip begins.

Imagine piecing together a 1,000-piece puzzle with no picture on the box—an analogy first brought to my attention by friend and colleague, Michael Witkowski. Putting together a puzzle without a box would be difficult and frustrating. You wouldn't know if you had all the pieces or even the wrong pieces to complete the picture.

Taking the time to understand where you want to go is much like painting the picture on the box. It gives you a clear idea of your direction and makes all future decisions much easier. When I work with folks, they have a lot of puzzle pieces, but often don't know what they're building. Putting together a vision for your life gets your feet moving in the right direction with clarity.

Understanding your goals is not just about money; it's about getting on a path where you feel more full and engaged with less stress. Imagine a life where you are just as excited about Monday as you are about Saturday. Set goals around outcomes and not about how much money you will earn. Stay focused on your values and the life you want to live.

I like to organize my thinking into four areas: spiritual, social, mental, and physical. Write those four headings down and start brainstorming. I call it my "post-it" note thinking session. Dream about what you want your future to look like. Let your mind go and begin writing down your goals and dreams. Have you always wanted to write a book? Do you want to travel around the world? Do you want to start a business? Do you want to volunteer more? Run a marathon? No idea is too big or small. Just write them down as they come to mind.

Once you have them on paper, take time to think more about them for a while and pray over them. Once I engage my mind on any problem, I often find that I will think of other things to add as I go about the tasks of my day-to-day life. When you think of something else, add it to your list. As you see your hopes and dreams written out before you, it will be easier to create steps to achieve them.

We sometimes don't give ourselves permission to dream when we are only focused on continuing down the path we're already on. Despite what we earn, it always feels like we need a little bit more, so our focus and effort go toward getting the next raise or promotion. Proverbs 23:4 puts it like this: "Do not wear yourself out to get rich; do not trust in your own cleverness." If you don't appreciate what you have now, then you will always sacrifice to get more. Whether it is your health, time with your family, or freedom to pursue other interests, you will find something must give in order to make room for the pursuit of money. Often, we spend the first half of our lives killing our health to gain wealth and the second half of our lives killing our wealth to gain health. What if we were able to find some balance along the way?

There was a woman who lived on a beautiful tropical island with her family. The woman was a potter who used the clay from the hills behind her home to make beautiful dishes with ornate designs on them. She loved the feel of the clay between her fingers and enjoyed the creative surge she felt whenever she fashioned something new. When she finished making her pottery, she sold it to friends in the village–making enough to support her family. On most days, she finished her work before noon and spent the rest of her time playing with her children, walking along the beach, and enjoying time with her husband. While the family was not rich, they were happy and content. They never lacked anything they needed.

One day a friend came to visit her. After looking around, the friend said, "Everyone loves your pottery! You need to do more. I can help you get rich and have a better life. You should move to a larger town and open a factory to make pottery. Instead of making pots, you can oversee people who will make them for you. You can sell those dishes and earn more money to be able to open more factories around the country. You will make millions!"

"How long will this take?" asked the woman.

"Maybe 20 to 30 years," the friend replied.

"What will I do then?" asked the woman.

"Oh, by then, you will be able to retire," said the friend. "You can relax and move away from the bustle of the city to a quiet island village. Once there, you can spend your days walking along the beach, enjoying your children and grandchildren, and pursuing your passion of working with clay."

I love how this story pokes fun at the rat race of life. We often get so caught up in wanting more that we don't realize we might work all those years to make money so that, in retirement, we can do what we could have been doing all along.

Let's suppose there are 10 things you need to find joy and fulfillment in life. Most people try to find a job that fills all 10. When their job meets only six of those needs, they start searching for another job. However, what if they found a great job which fulfilled six needs AND gave them time to do other things that would fulfill the remaining four needs? It's not just about money but about building margin in your life so you have time to do the things that give you fulfillment and purpose.

> **When everything is important, then nothing is important.**

So how do you get on the path to figure out your priorities and begin heading in the right direction? Many of us want it all. Everything is a priority. I want a nice house. I want to pay for my kid's college. I want to retire early. I want to travel. The list goes on and on. When everything is important, then nothing is important.

After working with several clients over the years, I've found the importance of learning how to *de-prioritize*. While everything seems important, some things are not as important as others. It is kind of like separating what is urgent from what is important. If everything on your list is always urgent (i.e. "I need to do this now or the world will end"), then you will never get to everything and the important things will remain undone. If everything is the most important then nothing is really a priority.

I had a couple come in one time that had a lot of financial goals and a modest income. To help them out, I wrote down the eight things they had mentioned that would most likely cost more than $50,000 during their lifetime. Note: this list is not a definitive list but an example a client might work toward on his or her own. To begin helping this couple to de-prioritize things, I asked the husband and wife to rank order the list separately. Then, I asked them to compare their lists and talk about why they ranked them the way they did and try to learn about what is important to each other. Here is the list I gave them:

1. Big/nice home (square footage, granite countertops)
2. Location of home (acreage, good neighborhood/school district)
3. Pay for children's college
4. Pay for children's private K-12
5. Give to church/charities
6. Have nice cars
7. Retire Early
8. Vacation Home

Once they finished this challenge, we sat and talked about the results and worked towards building a vision that they were both excited about. Later, my wife and I took this challenge with surprising results. We both put having a nice car at the bottom of the list and both valued paying for our children's education more than having a nice home. Once we did this, we realized we weren't focusing on the right priorities. We weren't saving anything for our children's education at the time because a good chunk of our money was going toward a large house.

It was difficult to give up what we already

had because it almost seemed like taking a step back. Yet, that is what we ultimately did!

We moved from the bigger house (which had an amazing kitchen) into a smaller home that had roughly half the square feet. Making the change helped us start saving for our children's educational future and do some of the other things higher on our list. While the big house had almost everything we wanted, there was a steep price to keep it. Downsizing gave us margin in our finances.

At first, giving up something we already had made us feel like we were failing. It felt like we were moving backward instead of forward. But in all reality, that wasn't true. We were just realigning our assets with our priorities. We were out of balance. To regain our balance, some changes had to be made. By focusing on the way we wanted to raise our children instead of the number of bedrooms, we were able to find a living situation that worked just right for us.

What was the result of making the move? There were definitely things we missed, but there were more things we gained. We always assumed our children each needed their own bedroom. However, when they didn't have their own separate spaces, they spent more time with the family because they only had one tiny, shared bedroom. The kids loved the closeness. Even when we later moved into a larger home and they had bedrooms of their own, they still had "sleepovers" in the other sibling's room because they enjoyed being together.

Also, because there was less space inside, we all spent more time outside. We love the outdoors, so being outside more was a real bonus. Of course, we also had more money freed up to pay for private K-12 Christian schooling and save for the children's college education. We could have "afforded" to stay in the large home, but what would it have really cost us?

If you want to accomplish your goals, you must be willing to sacrifice. You have to give up something you have in order to get something far greater. Like my wife and I in the example above, many people put having a nice car last on the list. When I drive our 10-year-old vehicle down the street, I am proud because, as it turns out, the intentional choice to hold onto our older car would help us achieve our dreams as a family. The extra money saved by not always having the latest and greatest car allows us to have a nest egg for our children's college education. Instead of an embarrassment, the car is now a symbol of the temporary sacrifices we made to accomplish our goals.

Personal Finance is PERSONAL. This book is about finding your Abundant Life and everyone has a different path to get there. Even as a couple, it is okay to be different. I asked a husband and wife once to "tell me about your ideal retirement." The wife went first and talked about traveling the world–she had loved being a stay-at-home mom but was ready to get out and have some adventures. When I asked the husband about his ideal retirement, he said, "I worked hard for 40 years. I'm looking forward to relaxing at home and playing some golf."

Even though he was planning on retiring in less than a year, they had never talked about what they wanted their life to look like, before or after retirement. We ended up making a Venn diagram of places around the world he'd want to golf and places she'd want to visit. She also had a sister that loved to travel. He was happy with his wife and her sister going together to some of the places he was not interested in traveling to.

Even something as simple as where you want to live is something many have not thought a lot about. When my wife, Angela, and I were trying to decide where to live, we ended up taking out a map of the United States. We sat down and discussed what was most important to us. For me, it was running my own business so I could have more autonomy and flexibility in my schedule and the freedom to coach my kids' sports. Being close to the mountains was also on my bucket list because I love to hike and be in nature. Angela wanted to be close to a beach since she loves the ocean. We both valued being somewhere that would be a good place to raise children and had good weather.

Because my wife is always cold, she drew a horizontal line across the map and said, "nothing above this line." After a bit of back-and-forth, we eventually decided to live in Raleigh, NC. We absolutely love it here!

We're about a two-hour drive from the beach and the mountains, our kids go to a great school, and the cost of living is wonderful. Unfortunately, we don't live close to our families in Minnesota, but we make time to travel to see them and they do the same. Again, life is about *trade-offs*. While this story is about physical location, you can see the power of taking a minute and thinking about the life you want to live.

It is always interesting to visit an estate sale and walk through beautiful homes full of stuff. Many times, things that were valued at thousands of dollars 20 years ago are now placed on a card table to be sold for a few bucks. While they seemed important then, no one even wants to buy them at a reduced rate. I sometimes wonder what fun memories could have been made had their assets not gone towards all this stuff.

Where are you heading? Stop, and pray about the direction of your life. Think about the things that are important to you and use them to set your current agenda. In the end, you will be glad you did.

For Reflection

1. Draw a picture of your future self and share it with someone. Don't worry about your drawing ability (or lack of it). You can include words and symbols to share the person you hope to become. What does the new you look like?

2. Have your own "post-it" note thinking session. Write down the words spiritual, social, mental and physical as your headers. Then, dream about what you want your future to look like. Let your mind go as you begin writing down your goals and dreams. Pray about your ideas and see what happens.

"Where there is no vision, the people perish: but he that keepeth the law, happy is he."

Proverbs 29:18 (KJV)

Chapter 5

Navigate Your Short and Long-Term Plans

Form a strategy and start working your way toward the goal. A goal without a plan to accomplish it is merely a wish. You need to figure out HOW you're going to get there because if you always do what you've always done, you'll always get what you've always got.

Appreciating what you have and believing *everything* belongs to God is foundational. It is like the footings that hold up the entire wall of your plan. However, at some point, you have to start making practical decisions about what to do with your life and consider how to manage the opportunities you have been given. Once you have that understanding, you can formulate a plan about where to go next. You will need to figure out where you are, where you want to go, and how you will get there.

My wife and I take a few days every year to get away from our daily routines and discuss our own life plans. Our parents take care of the kids while we put aside other obligations and go away for a short retreat together.

While away, we typically spend about four days having fun. Along the way, we carve out time to discuss our family routines, direction, and finances. It is much more fun to talk about goals when sitting around a pool or on a hike than at home being interrupted by the stress of everyday life. We take time to talk about our children. How can we help them grow into confident and capable adults who love God? We consider things like how we might help them better appreciate what they have. Are they at an age where a mission trip might be more important to their development than another beach vacation? How can we give more to those around us and at the same time help our children learn to become cheerful givers? We discuss whether I'm working too much and how I may be more present when home. Taking time to consider our plans each year helps us be more intentional in our daily lives rather than making random decisions that don't work toward our ultimate goals.

I like to think about our yearly goal-planning like shooting a bullet at the moon. Even if you aim really carefully (and had a gun that could shoot that far), by the time the bullet got there, if you didn't make any adjustments, you'd end up way off. Making adjustments along the way doesn't mean the goal changes. You are still aiming at the moon. Instead, you've only changed your tactics on how to get there. In much the same way, you must take time to make adjustments to your life plan as tactics and priorities change.

Once you have your goals in place, you must be patient. Most of the time, being successful is not about doing something extraordinary but rather doing something ordinary in an extraordinarily consistent way. Financial advisors often talk about the Rule of 72. This rule says 72 divided by your rate of return helps calculate how many years it will take to double your money. So, if you have a 7.2% rate of return, your money will double roughly every 10 years. From an investment standpoint leading up to retirement, the last 10 years of doubling (or compounding in this example) is worth as much as all the savings you've done your entire life. But, if you aren't patient to get to the end, you won't see that final prize.

Everyone wants to find a "get-rich-quick" scheme. Sometimes that does happen, but it's very rare and usually comes with significant risk. But more often than not, those that gain it all quickly lose it all just as quickly. Proverbs 13:11 says, "Wealth from get-rich-quick schemes quickly disappears; wealth from hard work grows over time" (NLT). Oftentimes, those who gain wealth suddenly don't have the wisdom or experience to make wise decisions about their newfound wealth.

There is comfort in creating a plan for yourself. For example, consider the stress and anxiety you feel if you are lost in the woods—maybe what started as a peaceful hike turned into something much worse than expected.

You don't have to panic and do wild and outrageously risky things to get home. Instead, you need to find and stay on the path. You get on the trail and keep going–trusting the path to lead you to civilization.

How many lottery winners have you heard of who won millions but are living in poverty a few years later? Often it is because they did not have a plan or purpose

> **Money, like time, walks away when we don't give it a job to do.**

for that money. Money, like time, walks away when we don't give it a job to do. By working a financial plan over time, you are more likely to achieve and maintain your goals. Trust the tried-and-true, long-term plan to get you there. Be patient—even if it takes a little longer to reach your end goal. It is ultimately the wisest course and ends up producing the most.

Warren Buffet once said, "The stock market is a device upon which to transfer money from the impatient to the patient." Many people buy impulsively at the high end and then sell when stocks are at the bottom of the market as they're trying to find the shortcut instead of staying on the path. Vanguard did a study on the value of an advisor and roughly half of the potential value was attributed to behavioral coaching (Kinniry, 2019). People often overestimate what they do in the short term and underestimate the value of their long-term actions. For instance, you could probably be in the top one percent of piano players in the world if you played 30 minutes a day for 10 years. It is the consistency over time that makes a difference.

Think about how many of us approach weight loss. We sprint the first hundred meters of the marathon (by trying to eat perfectly and work out more than a professional athlete) and quit from exhaustion before reaching the end. My dad was a doctor and once challenged me to focus on living a healthy lifestyle and ultimately, lose one pound per month. I told him that I could do way better than that. I disregarded his advice and lost 30 pounds that year. Unfortunately, the 30 pounds came from losing the same 10 pounds three different times and gaining it back each time! I ended the year at the same weight I had started. I frequently went all-in on diet and exercise plans that potentially worked in the short term but failed to have lasting success because they didn't easily fit into my lifestyle. I had made a goal of losing weight instead of living a healthy life. Dad urged me to be healthy and lose just one pound per month. In two years, I would have lost 24 pounds in a healthy way.

As you are heading down your path, be sure to make adjustments along the way. Author and Speaker Jon Acuff partnered with the University of Memphis to study how to help people complete their goals. Only about 8% of people accomplish their New Year's resolutions and Jon wanted to figure out how people could increase that number. Jon wrote: "the exercises that caused people to increase their progress dramatically were those that took the pressure off, those that did away with the crippling *perfectionism* that caused people to quit their goals" (Acuff, 2018). We can't let perfect get in the way of progress. For example, we have a goal of working out five days a week but miss the first three days. Instead of trying for the last four days of the week, we give up and say, "I'll just start next week."

We can't let perfect get in the way of progress.

I've yet to meet someone that hasn't made any mistakes financially. It is all about giving yourself grace and focusing on the next steps. Sure, there were some mistakes made. But you *must* navigate the plan. When a mistake happens, get back on the path and move forward.

I sometimes ask my kids, "Do you want to go on a vacation or do you want to go on an adventure?"

"Dad, we want an adventure!" they enthusiastically reply.

"Okay," I continue, "You know what makes it an adventure? It's because it is challenging and you will have both good and bad times. That's part of the journey. But the ups and downs make it a worthwhile endeavor!"

If you focus too much on doing everything perfectly, you will miss the joy of the adventure. Realize it is alright to make a few mistakes along the way. When you do make an error, take a moment to stop and reassess. Perhaps your bills are mounting and you don't have enough saved up to pay them. Maybe you have to sell something you bought and not get as much as you'd like for it. But doing so reduces your debts and stress from your life, getting you back on the path toward your future goals.

It is also important to build margin, or some "extra" into your plan. Many people live paycheck to paycheck, even if they have a good salary. Building margin and some conservatism—not needing a huge rate of return for your plan to work—helps the success of your plan and allows breathing room. Without margin in life, even the things you love lose luster because they are just adding to an already busy life. When circumstances are less than perfect (which they usually are), you will still succeed.

Working your plan takes constant readjustment. Along the way, you must follow your path, periodically check the map, and recalculate direction. Sometimes life's struggles seem overwhelming and it feels like you are retracing your steps. Often it is because you're on a treadmill rather than navigating the path God has planned. Be intentional in pursuing an abundant life and make adjustments along the way. Remember: it's the hills and valleys along the way that make life an adventure.

For Reflection

1. Plan a personal retreat to discuss your future. Where will you go to avoid distractions and focus on setting your future course? Is there someone that will go along with you to help plan?

2. People often overestimate what they do in the short term and underestimate the value of their long-term actions. What is one area of your life in which you would like to add more consistency?

3. It is all about giving yourself grace and focusing on the next steps. Mentally allow yourself to forgive your past financial mistakes and focus on your next steps.

"Be on your guard; stand firm in the faith; be courageous; be strong."

1 Corinthians 16:13

Chapter 6

Develop A Strategy for Risk

F ear can keep us from being our best selves or pursuing what God has planned for us.

One of the craziest risks I've ever taken was to jump out of an airplane *without* being tethered to an instructor. In the infinite wisdom of a person in their 20s, I decided the idea of putting my life in someone else's hands was too risky. Jumping by myself seemed to be a better choice. It was my first time skydiving *ever*, and so there I sat . . . in a small plane, hooked up to a parachute, and ascending to 13,000 feet.

As the plane rose, I looked out of the window and thought, "We must be about ready to jump." However, looking down at the altimeter on my wrist, I realized we had only reached 2,000 feet. We still had 11,000 feet to go! My heart dropped as fear set in. What was I thinking? Was I really going to do this? I had already paid for the skydive and spent three hours in a class learning the basics. Although my fear was rising, I was determined to jump out of that moving airplane!

When we finally reached 13,000 feet, the instructor opened the airplane door filling the cabin with a rush of air. For safety's sake, I was jumping alongside two other trained skydivers. All three of us had to step out of the plane onto a narrow platform beneath the wing. Like a caterpillar crawling on a side-walk, I inched out of the cabin clinging only to a pole attached to the plane. It was terrify-ing! My heart was in my throat, and my life seemed to flash before my eyes. This must be the end!

Finally, I opened my eyes and looked right. The guy gave me a thumbs-up. I looked left; that guy gave me a thumbs-up too. Following the instructions I'd been given in class, I pushed up to my tippy toes, crouched down, and jumped backward into the great unknown. It was one of the most vulnerable moments of my life. It all happened so fast. My hands and feet were flailing in the air. I looked at my companions who were giving me hand signals to straighten my legs more. Could I even do that? Yes. I unfolded my legs and continued falling seemingly faster.

As we got close to 5,000 feet, I looked at my altimeter and realized it was time to pull my ripcord. The instructors again gave me a thumbs up. I reached for the cord, and it wasn't there! Had they forgotten to put the cord on my parachute? Frantically, my hand searched up and down my waist. Where was the cord? At about that time, one of the instructors took my hand and placed it on the ripcord. Relief flooded through me. I grabbed it and yanked hard.

Suddenly, I flew up and began floating. It was amazingly quiet and peaceful, going with the wind like a bird. My companions were far below me because, while I'd pulled my ripcord at 5,000 feet, they pulled theirs at 2,000 feet and landed much sooner than I did. I'd looked at a map of the location where we were jumping before we took off. However, up in the air, I didn't have a map as a reference. I remembered we were supposed to land next to a small town. That made sense while I was looking at the map. But now, looking down amid the jump, I noticed TWO small towns. Which one do I land near? About that time, a voice came over the radio attached to me.

"Scott, you're drifting away from the landing spot. Cut to the right," the voice instructed.

The instructors coached me the rest of the way—steering me toward the true end goal. Finally, I made a safe landing. My adrenaline level was at an all-time high as my feet found the ground.

A year later, my wife and I decided to make a jump together. This time, we both went in tandem with our skydiving instructors, reducing the risk of the jump immensely. It was a much more thrilling experience to just focus on the joy of the journey versus worrying about all the technicalities myself.

As I've matured, I no longer have the

desire to skydive. Today I realize that some things just aren't worth the risk. This book is like the three-hour class taken before the skydive. You're getting some information but not enough to become an expert. Everyone is not at the same point in their lives. Some just need a little direction here and there to make sure they don't drift in the wrong direction. Others need a person to come alongside them and hold their hand to help them take action. While still others need to be strapped to someone else to make sure everything ends up alright.

Life is filled with risk and we are naturally designed to avoid it. In behavioral finance, there is a well-accepted bias called loss aversion. The loss aversion theory states that people tend to avoid loss because it is psychologically twice as difficult as the pleasure from an equivalent gain. For instance, you will feel roughly twice the pain from losing $10 than you will get pleasure from gaining $10. Because of this bias, we naturally take steps to avoid losses of any kind. Have you ever NOT applied for a better job because you feared rejection if you did not get the job? If you have never done this, you are better than most. It is so easy to choose inaction over action because of fear. The fear of rejection can be more powerful than the opportunity for a better life. More often than not, the easiest solution is to do nothing rather than develop a strategy to overcome the risk.

Don't fool yourself. The biggest risk you can take is not assuming any risk. You must develop a strategy to deal with the risk—it doesn't matter if you're just starting your career in your early 20s or are sending kids off to college in your 50s. In order to fly, at some point you have to take a leap of faith. During that leap, being aligned with what God has planned for you can make all the difference.

> **The biggest risk you can take is not assuming any risk.**

I think about the parable of the talents in Matthew 25. In the story, a man gave varying amounts of money to three investors. Two of them used the funds wisely, but one was afraid to take a risk. He was so worried he would lose money that he dug a hole and buried his treasure in the ground. He didn't lose money, but he didn't gain anything either. When the man returned, he was unhappy with the investor who used his resources unwisely and called him a "wicked, lazy servant."

As an investment advisor, one of the concepts I often talk about is developing a strategy to mitigate the risk. It is not about whether bad things will happen (because they will), but it is about what the consequences will be when things do go awry. We all wish we knew the future. Will we live a long time or die early? How much will taxes rise? When is the next market crash? These are the great unknowns. However, with good planning, you can develop strategies to mitigate even those risks. The risks that you do take need to be "calculated risks."

To accomplish your goals, you have to take risks to make them happen while trusting God to come alongside you. If you don't, you will never know the truly abundant life to which God has called you. It is risky to leave a secure position that you hate to start a job that you love. But you might mitigate the risk by building savings before quitting or by first developing a business on the side. There are typically multiple ways to get where you want to go. Many people stop moving forward because of the fear of the unknown. They are so afraid of losing the comfort of their current life they hesitate to start anything new. They fear asking the question, "What if...?" Yet, by overcoming that fear and developing smart strategies and plans, they can finally be free to take the leap of faith God has planned. When they do, they can finally start soaring!

As a sports fan, I love the Bible's account of David and the giant, Goliath, found in I Samuel 17. It is the ultimate underdog story where the little guy triumphs over almost insurmountable odds. While I love to think about David toppling that enormous giant, I also enjoy learning about what led up to the giant's fall. The giant's biggest strength was invoking fear in the people around him. Every day, for 40 days, Goliath came out and taunted the Israelite army while challenging them to a winner-take-all confrontation. The giant, who was close to eight feet tall, was so big that no one wanted to stand in his way. He could literally walk all over any one of them. The Israelites were terrified knowing that their world could be destroyed by the Philistine army. How could any Israelite warrior hope to defeat a giant?

Then David is introduced into the story. He is the polar opposite of the giant. He was just a boy–the youngest of eight sons–who wasn't even considered old enough to fight in the army. Yet David approached the situation differently. Rather than focusing on how BIG the giant was, David's thoughts centered on GOD. David recalled how God had shown faithfulness to him in the pasture. God had been with him as he wrestled sheep from the mouths of lions and bears. In comparison to God's greatness, Goliath looked small. David's great faith AND his strategy to overcome the giant helped him win the battle. David trusted God's guidance and used his wits to avoid hand-to-hand combat. With no armor and only five smooth stones and a sling, he took aim at the giant. With one powerful blow, he hit Goliath in the forehead. On the other hand, his much older and stronger brothers were paralyzed by fear and unable to engage in battle. They lacked faith that God would help them triumph and did not think outside the box when it came to fighting strategy.

Fear will often keep us from living our most abundant life. It holds us back from becoming the best version of ourselves. Fear causes our minds to make up a rendition of the worst-case scenario without considering the truth. Fear is often what keeps us back from financial success as well. We are so afraid of taking a risk that we do nothing. We don't make a well-thought-out investment because we fear the worst. We fail to understand we can't beat a giant if we don't take that first step toward him.

You might remember the New Testament story of Jesus feeding more than 5,000 people (Matthew 14:13-21). Through the multiplication of five bread loaves and two small fishes, Jesus feeds a crowd that had followed him to the wilderness. After this great miracle, Jesus sent his disciples ahead in a boat to cross the lake while he went to a mountainside to pray. The next morning, as the disciples looked out

from the boat, they saw Jesus coming towards them walking on the water. After just witnessing the great miracle of Jesus multiplying food, you might think that the disciples would be filled with faith and realize that Jesus could do anything. But that was not the case.

When they looked out and saw Jesus coming toward them, they thought he was a ghost. In that moment, their faith went overboard, and they sat motionless in the boat. However, one disciple, Peter, did things differently. Putting aside his apprehension, Peter asked Jesus to let him walk on the water toward him. When Jesus said, "Come," Peter stepped out of the boat onto the water. He began walking towards Jesus when suddenly he realized that what he was doing was impossible. He looked around at the fierce wind and waves, taking his eyes off Jesus. Suddenly, he began to sink.

Throughout history, Peter has received a lot of flack for his lack of faith in that moment. However, of all the disciples, he's the only one who took action and got out of the boat. He is also the only person, other than Jesus, that I know of that has walked on water. While he was not perfect, his faithfulness took him farther than all the rest.

Peter courageously walking on water reminds me that it is better to have tried and failed than to never have tried at all, communicated eloquently in the "Man in the Arena" speech given by former President Theodore Roosevelt in 1910:

> It is not the critic who counts; not the man who points out how the strong man stumbles, or where the doer of deeds could have done them better. The credit belongs to the man who is actually in the arena, whose face is marred by dust and sweat and blood; who strives valiantly; who errs, and comes short again and again, because there is no effort without error and shortcoming; but who does actually strive to do the deeds; who knows the great enthusiasms, the great devotions; who spends himself in a worthy cause; who at the best knows in the end the triumph of high achievement,

and who at the worst, if he fails, at
least fails while daring greatly, so that
his place shall never be with those
cold and timid souls who know
neither victory nor defeat.

If you avoid all risks, you will never
become the greatest form of yourself. The
author of Hebrews mentions men and women
who took action and stepped out in faith
(Hebrews 11). Each of these individuals is
only significant because they chose action
instead of inaction. Noah built an ark, even
when he had never seen rain, because he had
faith that God would send a flood. The
people of Israel had the courage to walk
through the Red Sea as if it were dry land.
Rahab, the prostitute, chose to welcome the
Israelite spies to her home even though her
neighbors didn't approve. They all took a risk
and trusted God to lead them forward.

There are countless other Biblical examples of those who are remembered because
they were not ruled by fear. How might
history have changed if Moses never led the
Jews out of Egypt because he was scared of

public speaking? What if David never stepped up against Goliath because he was not a soldier? Would Paul be remembered today if he had never preached for fear of prison?

What fears are keeping you from living an abundant life? I love how Philippians encourages us not to worry, but to experience God's peace: "Don't worry about anything; instead, pray about everything. Tell God what you need, and thank him for all he has done. *Then* you will experience God's peace, which exceeds anything we can understand. His peace will guard your hearts and minds as you live in Christ Jesus" (Philippians 4:6-7 NLT).

Trust that God has "got you," put aside your doubts and take a leap!

To mitigate fear, you must stop focusing on the worst that could happen and begin looking at the possibilities. Oftentimes, the worst-case scenario has a very low probability and may be something you can live with. If it is something you cannot live with, come up with a strategy to overcome the risk. Step out of the plane and jump; get out of the boat and begin to walk. You won't be able to eliminate the risk but you can lessen the possibilities of failure. Only by taking action and setting aside fear can you become what God has intended. Trust that God has "got you," put aside your doubts and take a leap!

For Reflection

1. What is the craziest risk you ever took? How did it work out for you?

2. What are you most afraid of losing in your current life that is making you hesitate to start anything new? What strategy can you put in place to mitigate the risk and take a leap toward your future?

"This is the day that the Lord has made; let us rejoice and be glad in it."

Psalm 118:24 (ESV)

Chapter 7

Acknowledge The Past. Find Joy in the Present. Prepare for the Future.

Have you ever met people who always seem to be reliving the glory days of the past? They tell stories of their high school sports accomplishments and the "good old days" as if nothing now, or in the future, could ever compare. On the other hand, have you met people who have so much former pain that it keeps them from moving forward with life? The difficult times have, in effect, made them stuck in their misery and unable to live a fully abundant life today.

You probably can see a bit of yourself in both of these people. Our memories, whether good or bad, sometimes seem to keep us from moving forward. We must acknowledge our past has shaped us into who we are today while not letting it rule our life.

I've never met anyone who had a perfect past. In fact, when we pause to reflect and really think about it, the "good old days" were not always as great as we remember. Sometimes we are quick to recall the positive events but forget the difficult ones. We remember the string of sporting events we won in high school, but forget the years of training it took and the relationships we missed out on to win those championships. Other times, the difficult events in our past are so big they seem to overshadow everything else. Our life seems to be encompassed by remembering the failed relationships, the loved one who died, the abusive home life, or a horrific incident.

We've all made mistakes with our finances, relationships, and life in general that we wish we could go back and change. Unfortunately, we don't get any "do-overs." We can't change our past no matter how much we try. But it is important to acknowledge our past *and* learn from it.

If you have never done so, you may need

to take time to sort out your past. You may be able to do this alone, but most people need someone to come alongside with whom to talk and help process. This may be a trusted friend, a mentor, or a spouse. Sometimes you may need a more experienced person like a professional counselor or psychologist. Whoever it is, they can help you learn from the past and then move forward.

I've already told you how getting cancer gave me a new appreciation for life, but it also created some roadblocks for me when trying to move forward. Although my doctor told me years ago my cancer was gone, in the back of my mind, I feared he was wrong. I had heard about others who were declared "cancer free" only to have the disease return later in a much more aggressive form.

While I wasn't afraid of dying and knew God had a plan for me, I wanted to ensure my family was taken care of if I were to die prematurely. Therefore, my life's focus was often on working hard and being a provider. I wanted to be certain my family would be taken care of financially after I was gone. However, what my wife and kids really wanted was for me to spend more quality time with them in the present. They longed for me to be with them while not worrying about work.

So, while I thought I had moved on from my life as a cancer survivor, I really hadn't. Deep down, there was a part of me clinging to the past. It was affecting the way I approached my day-to-day life. I had to think deeply about my fears, motivations, and actions to come to that conclusion. But when I did, I was finally able to address my fears and move forward accordingly.

In much the same way, our past can impact how we approach our finances. Often people are not educated on how to use money wisely. Many don't know how to handle money, but they think they do because they are following the pattern set by their parents. Their default is then to do what their parents did or the exact opposite–as that is the only education they've received on money. For instance, when I talk to some parents about helping their children pay for college, they will say,

"My parents didn't help me through

college, so my kids don't need any help either. I did it myself, so my kids can do it themselves too."

Other parents take the opposite approach.

"My parents didn't help me through college, so I'm going to make sure my kids get help."

Many don't realize their approach stems from their childhood experience. I find that even simple things, like the size and type of house in which they chose to live, are based on what their parents did or did not do years earlier. Only by fully realizing where their view is coming from can they put it in the past and move towards making the best decisions for their life.

If you are going to live a fully abundant life, you may need to take a moment and consider the hurts and pain of your past. What barriers from the past are getting in the way of living your most full and joyous life? What can you learn from the past that will help you live more fully? Are there people you need to forgive so the hurt they have caused doesn't take up so much space in your life?

On the other end of the spectrum, many people live too much in the future . . .

- *Once I get a bigger house, everything will be great.*
- *When I retire, my life will be fulfilled.*
- *Once I save a million dollars, I will have enough.*

Yet every time they reach the target, the goalpost moves and there is more to achieve. They work hard to climb the ladder only to learn it was leaning against the wrong wall. They don't realize if they are not happy now, they are probably not going to be fulfilled in the future either. They are so busy living in the future that they don't find happiness in the here and now.

While it is important to plan and prepare for the future, don't live there. It's the difference of living your life for the destination rather than the journey. A lot of people tell me they absolutely hate their job, but it is going to help them get the next job. Then, they get to the next job and find they don't like it either. Suddenly 30 years have passed and they never enjoyed their job. So, to an extent, they have put their hope in something that didn't actually bring joy. It is putting faith in money rather than God.

Living in the present acknowledges that joy is found in the journey–not just in reaching the destination. Being fully present allows you to enjoy the journey and focus on living it now. In Luke 10:38-42, Jesus visits the home of his friend, Martha, in the small town of Bethany. Martha, trying to be a good hostess, is busy making preparations for the evening meal. Meanwhile, her sister, Mary, sits at Jesus' feet listening to his words. Mary's seemingly inaction frustrates Martha– who believes that Mary is not doing her part to help with the household chores. Jesus reminds them both of what is truly impor- tant–being present with Him. I love the simple message of dwelling in the presence of Jesus and not getting caught up on all of the work that needs to be done.

Jesus taught us to live in the present

through the Lord's Prayer when he said, "Give us today our daily bread" (Matthew 6:11). Jesus meant not only bread but everything that we need to live. The prayer doesn't ask God to give us a never-ending supply of bread–just enough for today. God wants us to focus on today; tomorrow has enough worries of its own. Just for today, give us what we need. God will provide. Tomorrow will take care of itself.

If you've done the things we talked about so far to understand where you're going and make a plan to get there, you don't have to worry about the future. You can focus on executing your plan today. Focus on being present with the people around you. Just being there for the big and little pieces of life builds bonds and lasting memories.

After our wedding, my wife and I went on our honeymoon. We spent part of the first day taking pictures of anything and everything we thought we might want. Then we put our cameras away for the remainder of the trip. Instead of focusing on taking pictures for social media, we wanted to enjoy each other and be present in the moment.

No one is ever perfect living in the present. A few years ago, my daughter told me she loved going to the swimming pool with me more than anything else. I was encouraged to know she wanted to be with me but wondered why she liked being in the water so much more than spending time elsewhere. She quickly clarified it when she said it was because I couldn't have my phone with me in the pool. When we play together in the pool, I'm fully present. I'm not trying to capture a picture, answer an email, or look at a text. I'm just there playing with her (Now that is convicting!).

While my daughter's criticism was hard to hear, she was right. Since she loves arts and crafts, I asked her to make me a special box to store my phone in when I get home. Now my kids have "Box Power" to tell me to put the phone in the box whenever it becomes a distraction as I need a reminder now and then. Being with my kids is the most important thing in the world. Text messages come and go, but the time I spend with my children is what I truly cherish.

Being too busy will prevent you from

living in the present. Have you ever felt like a robot going through the motions of life? You wake up, go to work, eat dinner, watch television, go to bed, and then repeat the next day. You have so many important things pressing on you that you can't "stop and smell the roses." Jesus had this problem too. He had thousands of people wanting to be with him. Wherever he went, people would follow hoping to find healing and hope. Yet, the Bible tells us Jesus would find ways to get away to be still and pray. He would go to a mountainside or a garden to be alone. It's really hard for us to be still. We're so focused on go, go, go that we don't take the time just to be still. Yet if Jesus, in his infinite greatness, could find a way to stop and be quiet, then surely someone as simple as I am could do the same.

When I was in ninth grade at a Fellowship of Christian Athletes camp, I heard a speaker create an acronym for BUSY saying it stood for "Being Under Satan's Yoke." He said, "If the devil can't make you bad, he'll make you busy." Those words have always stuck with me. Don't let a busy life steal your joy and keep you from living fully in the present.

I once had the opportunity through a study abroad program to spend a summer in a small Italian town called Perugia. It was a picturesque hilltop village in the middle of Tuscany with stone streets, quaint church buildings, and lovely outdoor restaurants. In Italy, meals last for hours. My friends and I would go to dinner at about 6:00 p.m. and stay there until after midnight watching the people and enjoying the great food and fellowship. My favorite part of it all was there was no hurry. We just took time to enjoy the moment. I developed more close friendships during those drawn-out meals than I had with many other friends I had known for years back home.

At the end of the summer, I went back to Minnesota. I remember going out to dinner with friends a few nights after I returned. We ordered food, and after five or 10 minutes, one of my friends said, "What's taking so long?" I remember quietly thinking, "Is he so anxious to get away from me that he wants the meal to end as soon as possible?" Then, I realized it wasn't personal. He was just so used to the hustle and bustle of life in the U.S. that he found it difficult to slow down and enjoy the moment. Embrace and enjoy time with others without looking for the next big thing or trying to accomplish something else on your agenda.

As you're reading this book, take 10 long and deep breaths in and out. Your inclination may be to keep reading and get the book done as fast as you can. Instead, take time to relax. Start small and build on it. Get away from the busyness of life if only for a few moments. If you are burning the candle at both ends, you may not be as bright as you think you are. Keep in mind the future is a mystery and the past is history, but today is a gift, which is why they call it the present. Find ways to live it to the fullest.

For Reflection

1. Is there anything that happened in the past that is impacting you today? Is there a friend or counselor you can talk with to help sort out the past?

2. Are there people you need to forgive so the hurt they have caused doesn't take up so much space in your life?

3. How has being busy living in the future gotten in the way of finding happiness in the here and now? How will you overcome that?

4. How can being fully present allow you to enjoy the journey and focus on living it now?

"Each of you should use whatever gift you
have received to serve others, as faithful
stewards of God's grace in its various forms."

1 Peter 4:10

Chapter 8

Nurture Others

Find ways to think of others more than yourself. It isn't all about you. Jesus taught us not only to take care of ourselves but also to think about the needs of others.

After I had surgery to remove the cancerous lump in my neck, I stayed in the hospital to recover. That evening, my college roommates put on all of my clothes and walked across campus to come and see me. When I say all of my clothes, I mean ALL of them. They each put on about five shirts, several pairs of pants, and my boxer shorts on top. They looked ridiculous! Yet, they did it to show me they loved and supported me.

Keep in mind, I was diagnosed in the

second week of college, so I was not extremely close to any of them yet. I had met one of the guys at a summer camp and had just met the other two when I moved into the dorm. Despite having just met, they walked across campus, not caring what they looked like, to cheer me up. Their focus was not on themselves but on me. When they walked into my room, I felt so loved. It was scary coming out of surgery not knowing what was ahead. But their visit was like a jolt of joy getting me through a tough moment.

The abundant life means you don't have a cup half full or half empty; you have a cup overflowing. Abundance of joy flows into the service of others. It is a natural progression. God is the very nature of love. He made us in his image, so it makes sense we feel better when we are serving others.

Jesus' ministry was about serving others. Even though he was fully man and fully God, he didn't take advantage of his power (Philippians 2:6). Instead, he became a servant. He spent much of his ministry communicating this idea to his disciples. Unfortunately, they didn't always seem to understand. At various

times in the New Testament, we find
accounts of the disciples arguing among
themselves about which of them would be the
greatest. Who would get to sit right beside
Jesus when he became an earthly king? Even
the mother of the disciples James and John
got into a dispute urging Jesus to remember
her sons when he became the king (Matthew
20:20-23).

Jesus continued to teach and show his
disciples how they should live. His words
must have sounded almost contradictory to
them. Jesus said, "Anyone who wants to be
first must be the very last, and the servant of
all" (Mark 9:35). How can the last person end
up being first? What other king had spent his
life serving others?

During the final week of Jesus' life, he
demonstrated this concept to them yet again.
Jesus and his disciples got together to eat the
Passover meal together (John 13:1-17). The
Passover feast was especially significant to
Jewish people because it commemorated the
time when the Jews were slaves in Egypt.
Each year, during the feast, they recalled how
God had told them to sacrifice an unblem-

ished lamb and put its blood on their door-
posts. The night the ancient Jews followed
God's instructions, the angel of death came
through the land killing the firstborn son in
each home. However, the angel passed over
the households of the Jewish people who had
the lamb's blood over their doorways.

More than 1,300 years after the angel
passed over the doorways of the Jews, Jesus
and his followers gathered to worship and
remember the event. A sacrificed lamb and
Passover meal with unleavened bread had
been prepared for them. All good Jewish
people would have followed these same
customs every year. However, in the middle
of the rituals and normalcy, Jesus did something startling. He took a towel and filled a
basin with water. Getting down on his knees,
he washed the feet of everyone in the room
and dried them with a towel.

Footwashing was not unusual in the first
century. Most people wore sandals to walk on
unpaved roads and pathways. So, by the time
the day was nearing its end, their feet were
filthy. Before an important dinner, a servant
would often come in and wash everyone's feet

just like we might wash our hands before a meal. Rather than sitting at a table and chairs like we do today, Jesus and his disciples laid on their sides at a low table with each other's feet close beside.

While foot washing was familiar, it would have been unheard of for the host of the meal to do the foot washing. Menial tasks were a servant's job. Furthermore, it would have been totally unthinkable for a celebrity like Jesus to be the foot washer. When he got down on his knees to wash feet, everyone in the room was stunned. This was just not right!

But Jesus used this as a teaching moment. Rather than simply telling them how they should behave, he showed them with one demonstrative act. Then, he explained the significance of what he had done when he said:

"You call me 'Teacher' and 'Lord,' and rightly so, for that is what I am. Now that I, your Lord and Teacher, have washed your feet, you also should wash one another's feet. I have set you an example that you should do as I have done for you. Very truly I tell you, no servant is greater than his master, nor is a messenger greater than the one who sent him. Now that you know these things, you will be blessed if you do them" (John 13:13-17).

Jesus taught that humility is not thinking less of yourself but thinking of others more. He had a way of turning the disciples' understanding on its head. He became a servant so they could understand the nature of the love they were to have for one another. He knew they wouldn't completely understand what he was trying to teach them then, but he knew they would later.

After Jesus' death and resurrection, the disciples remembered what Jesus, the perfect Passover lamb, had taught and shown them. It was only later they fully understood his message. Peter talked about the Christian's life of service when he said: "Each of you should use whatever gift you have received to serve others, as faithful stewards of God's grace in its various forms" (I Peter 4:10).

Paul opens the letters of Romans, Philippians, Titus, and Colossians by calling himself a servant of Jesus Christ. The apostle John opened the book of Revelation by calling himself a servant (Revelation 1:1). Throughout the New Testament, the concept of Christian servitude is repeated over and over. Paul reminds Christians in the city of Philippi to take on the attitude of Jesus who humbled himself and became a servant. He reminds readers to "Do nothing out of selfish ambition or vain conceit. Rather, in humility value others above yourselves" (Philippians 2:3).

There are many ways we can show care and become servants to those around us every day. Maybe it is buying a cup of coffee for the person behind you at the drive-thru to bring a smile to their day. Perhaps it is raking leaves for an elderly neighbor or bringing food to a homeless person on the street corner. You may not ever know the impact, but you can change someone's life.

When I was a student at the University of Minnesota, I made an intentional effort to talk to people on my way to class each day. So, by the end of the semester, I was familiar with almost everyone I met along the way. However, one day I saw a girl I didn't recognize. I said hello and asked how she was doing. She said, "I'm fine." There was something in the way she said "fine" that didn't leave me with a good feeling.

"Tell me more. What's going on?" I inquired.

She gave me a strange look and said nothing.

"I know you don't know me," I continued. "It seems like something is wrong. It's okay. You can tell me."

"Honestly, a friend of mine just committed suicide. I was having similar thoughts."

"Do you want to talk about it? I can buy you a cup of coffee," I continued.

We ended up conversing for about three hours in a nearby cafe. At the end of our time together, we hugged and wished each other well. I'll never know the impact I had on her life. Just by showing concern and sincerely listening, our time together might have saved her life and it all started by asking a stranger how they were doing and actually caring.

Our lives are interconnected. You never know the impact you may have on another person by being there to offer support or believing in their dream when no one else seems to care. Maybe you'll change a child's future by volunteering to coach youth sports. Maybe you are a school teacher who shows up day-in-and-day-out. You may never realize the significance of doing your job purposefully and with a loving heart. Who hasn't had a teacher who made an impact on their future? The world needs people who will pour out their love into the world to make it a better place.

You have to be willing to go a little bit beyond just being nice and have the heart of a servant. My dad was a small-town doctor who took great care of his patients. He could have done enough during his regular office hours. However, he took one extra step. He gave out our home phone number. He told new parents, "feel free to call me at home if you have questions." In giving out his phone number, the extra step beyond nice made all the difference.

As a teenager, I remember many patients calling in the middle of the night asking for dad. He would listen and advise them about how to best care for their children. This was his ministry. He could reduce their worry and give them confidence in their parenting.

You don't have to do something big or heroic to make a difference. It is the little acts of kindness and love woven into our daily lives which can change the world.

One of my clients was turning 92 and mentioned none of her children were going to be with her to celebrate. A few days later, our Client Engagement Manager, Jennifer, drove an hour on a Saturday morning to take her out for breakfast. Jennifer didn't have to do this on her day off, but she decided to take an extra step to show love to someone who was lonely. Valuing her and making her feel special made all the difference. Years later, the client still talks about Jennifer's kindness in coming for her birthday.

Servitude is about investing in people, developing relationships, and being there for others. It is living out the words of Jesus when he said, "'For I was hungry and you gave me something to eat, I was thirsty and you gave me something to drink, I was a stranger and you invited me in, I needed clothes and you clothed me, I was sick and you looked after

me, I was in prison and you came to visit me'"
(Matthew 25:35-36).

One of the best examples of this type of servitude are two of my clients. They travel the country providing relief for those in the midst of disaster. They continually go into disaster areas and lend a helping hand. Together, they seem to be able to fix anything and always seem to know how to help. Although they felt called to serve in this way, there were several parts of their ministry they did not enjoy. One of their biggest struggles was their sleeping arrangements. Often, they did not get adequate sleep because their only option was to sleep on a nearby gym floor. In addition, one of their biggest priorities was to develop relationships with those they helped. This was frequently difficult because many of those they helped were busy during the day when they were working at their home.

Rather than give up their ministry, my clients worked to find a solution to the problems. They ended up buying a camper. Their home on wheels allowed them to sleep on site and have more time to get to know the families they were helping. Although the camper was expensive, they quickly discovered that it was an investment in their ministry and the people they serve.

While they served out of an abundance of joy, sometimes people help others out of a feeling of obligation. Their good deeds are a show for other people rather than a reflection of their hearts. This can lead to resentment and volunteer exhaustion.

I once heard a story about an American businessman who went to India for work. While there he heard Mother Teresa, the Catholic nun and founder of the Missionaries of Charity, was nearby. Wanting to meet someone famous, he went to see her. He watched as she and others selflessly served the poorest of the poor. He was so moved by this he wrote her ministry a check for an enormous sum of money.

When he gave the check to Mother Teresa, she ripped it up and said, "Go home, and love your wife."

On the plane ride home, he thought about her words. What did she mean? Why didn't she take my money? Don't I already love my wife? How can I do anything differently?

After pondering it, he realized he had been so caught up in the hustle and bustle of life he really hadn't been a great husband and father. While he told himself working hard and making lots of money was all for his family, he realized much of his work had been for his own pride and self-ambition. In a way, he had been "outsourcing" his good deeds by writing occasional checks. He realized his motivations for giving the money had been to help himself feel better rather than out of a desire to serve.

He decided right then and there to spend more time with his wife and son. Despite the long neglect, intentional engagement got them back on track sooner than he ever imagined. Later, he *and* his family returned to serve alongside Mother Teresa. This time he had the heart of a servant and his good deeds were from an abundance of overflowing joy.

If you want to make a difference in this world, you have to be different. You may not be able to change everyone, but you can find a few people in your part of the world to love and nurture.

This was Jesus' approach. Although he

had crowds surrounding him wherever he went, he chose 12 people, his disciples, with whom to build the closest relationships. He cared about everyone, but as a person, he couldn't be with everyone all the time. So, he chose only 12 people in whom to fully invest. He taught them so they could eventually go out and teach others.

> **If you want to make a difference in this world, you have to be different.**

These 12 men became the foundation of the church. After Jesus' death, resurrection, and return to heaven, they spread the gospel message all around the world. There was nothing innately special about these men. They had regular jobs, such as fishermen and tax collectors. They had parents, wives, and families. But what distinguished them was their willingness to follow Jesus. They spent time and learned from Him. Then, using what they learned, they went out and nurtured others.

Using your gifts draws you closer to God. My wife loves to sing. She sang in choirs for many years and now uses her voice to lead worship at our church. While she blesses those who hear her sing, she receives the greatest blessing as she uses her gift. I find the same thing is true with my financial planning. When I can use my skills to help someone else find their life's plan, I am often encouraged and fulfilled even more than they are.

How can you find a way to serve? Look around you. You might want to join others in an existing ministry or perhaps you will start your own. Many churches showcase different opportunities each week. You won't be able to do everything, but, by seeing the need, something may tug at your heart.

Listen to your heart. What is the first thing coming to mind when you think about serving? Will you serve with your time, talent, treasure, or all three?

One of my best friends from high school, Michael Swalley, listened to his heart, and it has taken him all over the world. After college, Michael did an internship for Focus on the Family in Australia. In his off time, he focused on a hobby he was passionate about: breakdancing. As he got to know the other breakdancers in the Hip Hop community, he found that many came from fatherless homes and previously had a negative experience with the Church. Seeing an opportunity to combine his passion for breakdancing and ministry, he started Break Free Ministries in southern California. Now, his non-profit has 28 missionaries in 11 cities and six different countries that are reaching thousands of young men in the Hip Hop community to stop the cycle of fatherless homes and introducing them to Jesus.

Sometimes the biggest struggle you have overcome can become your best ministry.

Break Free Ministries succeeded from the start because Michael is an amazing breakdancer that could relate with a shared interest. It has flourished because Michael has a unique ability to connect with those who do not have a father because he grew up without his father. Sometimes the biggest struggle you have overcome can become your best ministry. When someone receives a cancer diagnosis, I can understand better than most because I have been through it. While I didn't want to get cancer, God has been able to use my experience to bring help and healing to others. Cancer has taught me I can't control everything. I'm a better person because I've been through hard times.

What's something tough you've overcome? How can you help someone else get through something similar? Many of the world's greatest ministries were started in response to great pain. For instance, Celebrate Recovery is a ministry that was born out of the founder John Baker's addiction to alcohol. To date, it has helped over seven million people with addictions walk in freedom through the power of Jesus Christ. Celebrate Recovery encourages people to find their identity in Jesus Christ and aims to bring healing and restoration to individuals and families whose lives have been fractured by hurts, hang-ups, and habits. Its success is greater because of the struggle that John faced on his own journey.

Maybe you think you can't change the world. It is too difficult to find the time to give to others. Take heart! It is not about disciplining yourself to give. Rather, as you go upstream and draw closer to God, you will want to give as God has given to you.

David talks about this concept as an overflowing cup in the 23rd Psalm. Nurturing others is the natural progression of feeling content and having an excess of love in your life. If your cup is overflowing, then don't waste the overflow. Give it to someone else. Nurturing others from your overflowing cup will bring you more joy than you can ever imagine.

For Reflection

1. If you have one hour this week to help somebody else, who will it be?

2. Think about a cause you're passionate about. How can you devote more time to helping this cause move forward?

3. Can you recall an incident in your life when someone else brought you a "jolt of joy" to get you through a tough moment? How can you share that same joy with someone else?

4. What's something tough you've overcome? How can you help someone else get through something similar?

"As iron sharpens iron, so one person sharpens another."

Proverbs 27:17

Chapter 9

Take Time For the People in Your Life

Imagine everything went exactly as you wanted financially but you had no one to share it with. Would it be worth it? People aren't meant to be alone; they are designed to live in a community. Everyone needs the love and care of those around them.

In prison, one of the worst punishments is solitary confinement. Being alone for long periods of time without meaningful contact with others can drive someone crazy. There are so many negative side effects of leaving people alone for long periods that many laws have been put in place to restrict the number of days that prisoners can be left alone.

John Donne, a writer from the seventeenth century, talked about our need for each other when he wrote the poem, "No Man is An Island." He said that rather than being like an island, people are like a huge continent–all connected and each affecting the other. If one person dies, then everyone is diminished because we are all connected.

Researchers from Harvard conducted the longest psychological study in history on the factors that drive human happiness. During a 79-year study, they followed 700+ men and explored what made them happy (Mineo, 2014). Was it a supportive spouse? Great job? Lots of money?

At the end of the study, they concluded quality relationships with family and friends were the number one indicator of a person's overall happiness. Life is tough. People who have someone else to help them through difficult times have more satisfaction. Also, it helped to realize they were not alone–other people experience hard times too. Helping another person weather the tough times brings purpose to life. Robert Waldinger, director of the study, said while relationships aid in the pursuit of happiness, the alternative is that "loneliness kills." He likened the power of loneliness to smoking or alcoholism.

The Bible supports the idea that we are meant to live in community. At the beginning of time, God created both Adam and Eve saying it was not good for people to be alone (Genesis 2:18). Just as a strand of three cords together is not quickly broken, a group of people can accomplish more than an individual (Ecclesiastes 4:12). Together, they can weather the hard times much better than we ever could do it alone.

Jesus taught that our relationship with God is both vertical and horizontal. We connect with God vertically through prayer or scripture, but we express and strengthen our relationship with God by reaching out to the people around us. Over and over, Jesus reiterated that true joy can be found by loving other people. In John 15:12, Jesus said, "This is my commandment, that you love one another as I have loved you" (ESV). The apostle Paul reminds Christians living in the region of Galatia to, "Carry each other's burdens, and in this way you will fulfill the law of Christ" (Galatians 6:2).

I have been fortunate that my family, along with my wife's family, are amazing people that are supportive and fun to be around. I recognize that not everyone is so fortunate. It is important to find the right people with whom to surround yourself. Throughout my life, I've had friends who seem to bring out the best in me. Being with them makes me so much better than when I am apart from them.

In much the same way, I think of this as a parent. How do I bring out the best in my children so they can thrive? Can I connect with them in ways that will help them become all that God has planned for them?

While it is important to spend time with your immediate family, it is also crucial to make friends with others outside your family group. I have found that young parents don't reach out to others because they are too busy raising a family. Children's needs seem to constantly tug at you. But, it is important to spend time with other adults.

I met one of my best friends when we

both lived in California. We played basketball together every Saturday morning and spent time talking afterward. We both own small businesses and found that we faced many of the same struggles. Our children are similar ages and our wives enjoyed spending time together. It was a fun and easy relationship where we built each other up.

Eventually, we both moved away. Today, I live near Raleigh, NC, and he lives near Boise, ID. Although spending time together isn't as easy as it once was, we still find a way to connect. Whether it is taking time to share a thought through text or having a long phone conversation, maintaining our relationship is important to us as we build each other up. We both know that we have a friend, even through the long distance, that will hang with us through the tough times.

I have always been a talkative person who thrives on spending time with people. When I am with others, my energy level seems to soar. Even my children seem to recognize this particular aspect of my personality. Once, I was in the middle seat on an airplane with my wife and two children (ages 4 and 6 at the time) sitting in the three seats directly in front of me. My daughter turned around and looked at me over the seat back. In a sweet little voice she announced loudly, "Daddy, you're sitting next to strangers! You LOVE to chit-chat with strangers, so you're really going to have fun on this flight!" I could almost hear the people next to me cringe and think, "Oh great, I'm sitting next to a talker."

While I tend to surround myself with people, developing close friendships is something that I have really had to focus on. I remember reading a tweet that asked "Who are your 2 a.m. friends?" These words made me stop and think. Who would I be comfortable calling if I needed something in the middle of the night? Even more, who would have me on their list to call if they were overwhelmed at an inconvenient time? Had I developed close friendships or do I just have a bunch of casual surface-level friends?

During college, I created my "Midnight Ministry." Since I don't need much sleep, I told friends they could always call if they needed anything in the middle of the night. I turned up the volume on my phone so I could hear when they called, just in case I was actually asleep. Through the years, I received a lot of calls. One of the biggest issues people called about was relationships. So, I developed my own relationship theory to help them through the tough times.

My theory was that there are four steps in a healthy relationship. The first step, which usually happens rather quickly, is to care about the other person. The second is to trust the other person with your heart and your actions. The third is to love them and self-sacrifice for their benefit. Finally, being around them makes you a better person.

In poor relationships, the fourth step didn't happen. One person might make the other better but not vice versa. Ultimately, the relationship was imbalanced so it didn't last or the couple took a step backward. Do you only pray for blessings or do you pray and yearn to be a blessing to others? Are you encouraging others? Are you going deeper with your friends?

Jesus was our great example of cultivating close relationships. While he spoke to the masses, he focused on just 12 individuals–his apostles. He went deeper rather than wider. Sometimes I feel like I have a lot of friends because I have hundreds of "friends" on social media and a bunch of casual friends, but I believe it is important to invest in close relationships. The kind of friends you can trust to tell your deepest, darkest secrets. We all need those strong, close relationships whether it is with a spouse, family member, or co-worker. Like Jesus, be intentional about building a few close relationships.

When I got married and had kids, life got insanely busy. I was focusing so much on being a great husband, parent, and employee that I let some of my other relationships slide. Some days it was all I could do to get through work and spend time with my family. The people around me all seemed to be in a similar situation. How could we possibly find time to develop deep friendships outside my immediate family in a hectic world?

I've found that it is not easy, but it is not impossible either. Carving out time in your schedule is the first step. If there is no margin, or free time, in your life, then how will you make friends?

I'm a huge believer in hard work. One of my life verses is Colossians 3:23, which says, "Whatever you do, work at it with all your heart as working for the Lord, not for human masters." Whenever we think about hard work, we tend to apply it to our careers. However, "Whatever you do" includes building relationships, not just your occupation. So it takes effort and planning for me to have some fellowship with my friends.

Life always has its ebbs and flows. There will be busy times when I need to work more and won't have much time for my friends. However, there needs to be less busy times too. None of us are ever going to be a perfect friend and we need friends that understand that as well. We can't spend every moment of each day together, but we can find small ways to spend time together to allow relationships to grow. Build margin into your life so you have time to be a friend to those around you.

I love the neighborhood I am in as it is full of amazing people. When I enter my neighborhood, I always take the long way to get to my house because I pass more of my friends' houses, which allows me at times to check in and see how they're doing. We even have a group of dads in our neighborhood that will load up in a minivan and go hang out periodically.

The house I bought in the neighborhood didn't have any grass in the backyard when we purchased it—it was all leaves and pine needles. My wife and I, being Northerners, wanted green. So, we ordered 20 cubic yards of dirt as a base for the grass. As soon as two full dump trucks dropped dirt on our driveway, the forecast changed. It was going to rain the next day.

I was working as hard as I could to put shovelfuls of dirt in the wheelbarrow and push it to the backyard. However, despite my aggressive perspiration, it felt like I wasn't making a dent.

They saw my struggle and jumped right in without hesitation.

A few neighbors saw what I was doing and graciously offered their assistance. By the end of the day, the job, which had seemed insurmountable when we started working, was completed. We never would have made it without their help. The servant hearts they demonstrated helped strengthen the connections with those neighbors. At the end of the day, we pulled out the grill and lawn chairs to have a big barbecue. It is a simple but beautiful example of what living in a community looks like. The best part was that I did not need to ask for help; they saw my struggle and jumped right in without hesitation. I bet you wish you had neighbors like mine. The funny thing is your neighbors wish they had neighbors like mine and you can be that neighbor!

Be intentional about building strong and healthy relationships. Find people who you enjoy and that make you a better person. Whether it is helping a neighbor with a project or going out together for dinner, find ways to cultivate a few close friendships.

Relationships aren't built in a day—it takes both time and intention.

Surround yourself with healthy, encouraging people. A solid support system is extremely important. It isn't whether you will go through tough times but about when that will happen. When it does, having a team to support you is essential. If you spend time with the right people, they encourage you and bring out your best. Relationships aren't built in a day–it takes both time and intention.

After I moved to the Raleigh area, I eventually became business partners with David Calloway. We built our business around helping others together. We both truly cared about those we served, and we had complementary skill sets. David and I had so much fun working together. We often jokingly told others that when we were together, $1+1=3$. Together we grew our business by more than three times within three years.

Our friendship went deeper than just a work relationship. I remember the time when David and I were at a work conference in Orlando, and I received word that my grandmother had passed. I was very upset by the news as we were close. I had driven down to Orlando because I wanted to visit some friends along the way; David had arrived by plane. When I told him about my grandmother, he realized what a big loss this was for me. When the conference was over at 9 p.m. that Saturday, I decided I just wanted to get home. Instead of merely saying he was sorry and understood, he took action. He canceled his plane reservation and drove 9 hours home with me so I wouldn't have to be alone.

David was an early-to-bed, early-to-rise kind of person. But that night, he stayed up all night, keeping me awake, so I could continue to drive and get home to my family. We talked, laughed, and kept driving. Whenever I would start to feel drowsy along the way, David would yell "freeze out." We'd open the car windows and let the cool January air rush over our faces. I'll never forget his kindness. He was there for me when I needed it the most.

A few years later, David was diagnosed with cancer and passed away at the age of 65. I was devastated by that loss, but I know I am a better person for having had him in my life. I hope that I can be the kind of friend to others that David was to me.

David's passing reminded me of how fragile life can be. As a result of that reminder, I have made a more intentional effort to spend quality time with my parents. For my dad's 72nd birthday, I took him to the infamous Penn State "white out" college football game as they were playing my beloved Minnesota Gophers. While the atmosphere was amazing to see over 106,000 fans dressed all in white, cheering loudly, the best part for me ended up being the 16 hours we spent together in the car. We talked about life, discussed parenting, and had some fun along the way (like stopping in Hershey, PA to get some chocolate). I'll always remember that trip; spending time with my dad is one of the best investments I could make for my well-being and fulfillment in life.

> **The greatest things in life aren't things but the memories you create with the ones you love.**

You'll never know the fullness that you can experience just by spending time with other people. I've come to realize that it is those relationships that are most important. I sometimes consider what I will value when I am dying and looking back on my life. Will I have regrets and wish I had lived life differently? I hope not. I want to make time now for the people in my life. The greatest things in life aren't things but the memories you create with the ones you love.

For Reflection

1. When have you had a friend or family member be there for you in a tough time? When have you been able to be there for a friend or family?
2. List a few people with whom you plan to build a closer relationship.
3. What are some ways that you have found to build closer friendships in our hectic society?

"May the God of hope fill you with all joy and peace as you trust in him, so that you may overflow with hope by the power of the Holy Spirit."

Romans 15:13

Chapter 10

Live Your LIFE with Joy

The journey begins with the first step. Remember you don't need to be rich to live a rich life. Rather, stop and think about what brings you joy. Make a plan to live a life focused on your purpose and use money to help fulfill that purpose. If you do, then life can be much fuller and less stressful.

When my wife, Angela, and I were dating, I often bought her expensive gifts. Her words of affirmation and encouragement after receiving them made me feel good and want to give her more. Here is how the process played out. I would give a nice gift, then she would enjoy it and respond in a positive way. I felt good about myself and our relationship.

THEN, we got married, and suddenly things changed. I kept doing the same thing I had done before. I'd spend a lot of money on a gift for her. But now, she responded differently. She didn't seem as excited about it or give me words of encouragement. What was the problem? It must be that I didn't get her a big enough gift, right? So, the next time, I got her something bigger and spent even more. Again, the response was the same.

Angela and I got engaged six months from the day we first met (if you know, you know) and got married about six months later. Because we got married so quickly, we had decided beforehand that we'd go see a couples counselor six months after we were married. From there, if either of us ever wanted to go back, we'd go back without any questions.

Roughly six months after our wedding, we went to see a counselor who asked why we had come. We described how we had married a few months earlier, had never argued, and were happy newlyweds. But, looking forward, we wanted to equip ourselves with relationship tools.

The counselor began with the topic of money and asked Angela a series of questions. The first few centered on Angela's thoughts about money and spending. It was very interesting to hear, but then he began asking her about what she thought MY theories were about money. As I listened, I tried hard not to interject. How did she get me so wrong? In short, it wasn't long before we had our first argument in the counselor's office. After more discussion, I finally understood what was bothering Angela about my gift-giving. The problem was now that we were married, I was spending OUR money instead of MY money. I kept giving bigger and bigger gifts in hopes of getting words of encouragement. Instead, I was stressing her out by spending money on her that she felt was needed elsewhere.

On her next birthday, I bought her a vase and filled it with 100 little hearts I cut out from colorful paper. On the front of each heart, I wrote a reason that I loved her. I included a note about Sonnet 43, "How do I love thee, let me count the ways...." The pastor had read these words at our wedding. Although I spent a lot of time on this gift, it didn't cost very much money. It turned out to be so much more meaningful than the fancy gifts I had bought her before.

Having that conversation relieved a lot of stress for us both. Now we don't buy gifts for each other that cost more than a certain amount without talking about it first. Since then, our gifts to each other have been more creative and meaningful. We both get more joy from the giving and the receiving than ever before, especially as we focus on experiences more than stuff.

The concept here is to stop and think about what brings you joy and what stresses you out. Make a plan to focus on what brings meaning to life rather than just on earning (or spending) more and more.

Everything is connected. The decisions you make today matter. If you aim at nothing, you will hit it every time. Without intentionality, time will fly by and stress will prevail! Understanding your future vision is not just about money. It's about getting on a path where you feel more full and engaged.

Are you ready to make your plans for the future? If so, start by taking time to think about and appreciate what you have. What are the many blessings in your life? Take time to pray and thank God for even the small ways that He is working through you. Then, take a look at the biblical foundations of your life. Understand that you are a caretaker of the abundance that God has given. If everything in your life is on loan to you for a time, consider how you will maximize those opportunities.

Take time to decide where your life is headed. Most people don't start on a journey without knowing their destination. Think about and map out your life's direction before you get much further down the road. Taking these steps at the beginning is so important to make sure you are on the path toward an abundant life. Once you know where you are heading, start laying out your short and long-term plans. Dream big. If you could do anything in life, what would it be? How can you make that happen?

I was blessed to volunteer with Saddle-back Church based in Lake Forest, CA, as they worked on their PEACE Plan as a Global Initiative. Talk about thinking big! They dreamed of Christians working together to transform the world. They started by working through the churches in the impover-ished nation of Rwanda. They had an orphan initiative that focused on helping kids in orphanages be placed in forever families. Through their unified efforts working along-side local churches, Rwanda went from about 100,000 children living in orphanages to under 3,000, with only two orphanages left in the entire country. Without short and long-term plans and thinking BIG, these children would not have found homes. It is hard to realize the impact a group of Christians, working together, can make on the world. What plans can you make today that will change the world tomorrow?

As you develop those plans, understand that you will need to navigate through the different challenges. No one succeeds 100% of the time. Albert Einstein once said, "Failure is success in progress." This concept works for the actions you take both personally and financially.

When you *do* leap and make a big transition in life, make sure you have a good team alongside to encourage and help you make wise choices and mitigate risk. Proverbs 15:22 says, "Plans fail for lack of counsel, but with many advisers they succeed." Perhaps you can partner with trusted tax experts, realtors, insurance agents, or estate attorneys to help make sound decisions financially. A physical trainer or workout buddy can also help you stay in shape and maintain a healthy balance mentally and physically. Spiritually, you may find a pastoral team to help as you seek God's purpose for your life. A Bible study group or an accountability partner (that you can be 110% honest with your deepest struggles) could also be an important part of the team.

Consider having a wealth advisor as the financial team quarterback. There are many amazing advisors who may be able to help. Some have designations, while others do not. Look for someone with experience to become the best fit for you. Here are a few items to watch for when seeking someone to direct your team.

A "CERTIFIED FINANCIAL PLAN-NER™" designation is a professional certification with rigorous ethical standards that is earned by financial professionals who have completed its extensive training and experience requirements. If you are a Christian, I would encourage you to also seek out an expert who has training as a "Certified Kingdom Advisor®" aligning their technical expertise with biblically wise counsel for their clients. Christian financial advisor legend Ron Blue's teachings through the Kingdom Advisor program have been instrumental in my development as a wealth advisor. An advisor should also serve as a fiduciary. That means their primary goal is to help make decisions in the client's best interest. Of course, you will want to find someone who listens to where you are trying to go and helps you get there.

An excellent advisor understands there is greatness in you and helps to bring it out. While there are great financial consultants who don't have all of these qualifications, looking for these credentials can be a great first step in selecting an advisor. Find someone who will come alongside you and encourage you to do the things for which God has called you. Like my skydiving experience, the journey will be much less stressful if tethered to an expert. A Vanguard study showed that when people worked with an advisor, their "peace of mind" went up 56% (Costa, 2022). The goal of a financial planner is to help you understand where you're trying to go, get you on a path to get there, and help mitigate risk along the way so you can engage in your passions, serve others, and be active.

Next, remember to look at your plans and consider why you are planning that way. Acknowledge the past and how it impacts your future. Find ways to nurture others and find meaning through those encounters.

In law school, I got certified in Family Law mediation. Before becoming a wealth advisor, a team member I worked with was on the brink of divorce. I offered to help his family with their finances, believing it could be causing conflict in their marriage. As we met together, I gave both partners five uninterrupted minutes to share their feelings and stress. I encouraged them to use "I feel" statements rather than attacking each other and pointing out the other person's faults. Turns out, both felt stressed about their finances and wanted change. However, the constant stress kept them fighting each other most of the time.

After a few meetings together, they realized they were each repeating the mistakes of their parents. They decided to be bold enough to do something different, and together, they started rowing their boat in the same direction and found balance, momentum, and then success. They eventually each became the first person in their families to own a home. Ten years later, this couple is still together and thriving. It was from their experience I decided to become a financial advisor to help lead others on a path toward a better life.

Above all, make time for positive people and relationships in your life. Realize that the joy is in the journey...not only in reaching the destination. We sometimes focus so much on the end goal that we miss the wonderful moments along the way, which make it all worthwhile. We can't wait to get married, have children, or retire. While these are important milestones, life is filled with a million other little things to appreciate. Live every day like it is your last. Appreciate the moment–not wishing it away. Make your goal to make every day more fulfilling than the last.

Are you living the life you have always wanted? Don't wait for a cataclysmic life-changing moment to make needed changes in your life. Let this be your wake-up call as tomorrow is not promised! Start building now toward your abundant life. The journey is amazing and worth the effort and intentionality. You're going to love it! I hope that you will find that life is more amazing than you ever dreamed as you start living in it and building toward it. Enjoy the adventure!

Journey Towards An Abundant Life

1. **A**ppreciate What You Have
2. **B**elieve Everything Is God's
3. **U**nderstand Where You're Headed
4. **N**avigate Your Short and Long-Term Plans
5. **D**evelop a Strategy for Risk
6. **A**cknowledge the Past. Find Joy in the Present. Prepare for the Future.
7. **N**urture Others
8. **T**ake Time for the People in Your Life
9. **LIFE**–Live Your LIFE with Joy

For Reflection

1. Who are the people that you are going to take along on your journey?
2. How will you surround yourself with encouraging people that can be part of your strategy for success?
3. Dream big. If you could do anything in life, what would it be? How can you make that happen?
4. After reading this book, which of the A-B-U-N-D-A-N-T areas are you going to focus on first?

Works Cited

Acuff, J. (2018). *Finish: Give yourself the gift of done*. Portfolio/Penguin, p. 4.

Costa, P., & Henshaw, J. E. (2022, February). *Quantifying the investor's view on the value of human and robo-advice*. Retrieved December 3, 2022, from https://www.vanguardmexico.com/content/dam/intl/americas/documents/mexico/en/2022/02/mx-sa-2056467-quantifying-the-investors-view-on-the-value-of-human-and-robo-advice.pdf

Donne, J. (2022). *Meditation #17 By John Donne From Devotions upon Emergent Occasions* (1624), *XVII*: Retrieved December 3,

2022, from https://genius.com/John-donne-meditation-xvii-annotated

Kinniry, F. M., Jaconetti, C. M., DiJoseph, M. A., & Zibering, Y. (2019, February). *Putting a value on your value: Quantifying Vanguard Advisor's Alpha.* Retrieved December 3, 2022, from https://www.google.com/url?q=https://www.vanguard.ca/documents/quantifying-your-value-research.pdf&sa=D&source=docs&ust=1670099031665331&usg=AOvVaw0HUuGYtQE4bhFk9gx_LvaU

Mineo, L. (2018, November 26). *Over nearly 80 years, Harvard study has been showing how to live a healthy and happy life.* Harvard Gazette. Retrieved December 3, 2022, from https://news.harvard.edu/gazette/story/2017/04/over-nearly-80-years-harvard-study-has-been-showing-how-to-live-a-healthy-and-happy-life/

Roosevelt, T. (1910, April 23). *Citizenship in a Republic: The Man in the Arena* [Paper Presentation]. Speech at the Sorbonne, Paris. Retrieved January 18, 2023, from https://www.leadershipnow.com/tr-citizenship.html

Disclosure

The opinions expressed by Scott Ferguson in Living The Abundant Life are for general information only and are not intended to provide specific advice or recommendations for any individual. To determine what may be appropriate for you, consult with your attorney, accountant, financial or tax advisor prior to investing.

Investment advisory services offered through CWM, LLC, an SEC Registered Investment Advisor. Carson Partners, a division of CWM, LLC, is a nationwide partnership of advisors.

JD is an educational degree and holder does not provide legal services on behalf of Abundant Life Financial or its affiliates.

Office Address (at time of publication): 5540 Centerview Dr, STE 418; Raleigh, NC 27606